First World War
and Army of Occupation
War Diary
France, Belgium and Germany

60 DIVISION
181 Infantry Brigade
London Regiment
2/24 Battalion
24 June 1916 - 30 November 1916

WO95/3032/9

The Naval & Military Press Ltd
www.nmarchive.com
Published in association with The National Archives

Published by

The Naval & Military Press Ltd

Unit 10 Ridgewood Industrial Park,

Uckfield, East Sussex,

TN22 5QE England

Tel: +44 (0) 1825 749494

www.naval-military-press.com

www.nmarchive.com

This diary has been reprinted in facsimile from the original. Any imperfections are inevitably reproduced and the quality may fall short of modern type and cartographic standards.

© **Crown Copyright**
Images reproduced by permission of The National Archives, London, England, 2015.

Contents

Document type	Place/Title	Date From	Date To
Heading	WO95/3032/9		
Heading	60th Division 181st Infy Bde 2-24th Bn London Regt Jun-Nov 1916		
Heading	181st Brigade 60th Division Battalion Disembarked Havre 25.6.16 2/24th Battalion London Regiment (The Queens) 24th June To 31st July 1916		
War Diary	Warminster	24/06/1916	24/06/1916
War Diary	Le Havre	25/06/1916	25/06/1916
War Diary	St Pol	26/06/1916	26/06/1916
War Diary	Chelers	27/06/1916	06/07/1916
War Diary	Maroeuil	07/07/1916	07/07/1916
War Diary	Ecurie	08/07/1916	12/07/1916
War Diary	In The Line	13/07/1916	16/07/1916
War Diary	Etrun	17/07/1916	19/07/1916
War Diary	In The Line	20/07/1916	28/07/1916
War Diary	Ecurie	29/07/1916	31/07/1916
Operation(al) Order(s)	2/24th Battn. London Regt March Order No.1	05/07/1916	05/07/1916
Miscellaneous	Battalion Order In The Field By Lieut Colonel J.P.G Crosbie Cmdg 2/24th Battn London Regt. The Queen's	12/07/1916	12/07/1916
Miscellaneous	Battalion Order In The Field By Lieut Colonel J.P.G Crosbie Cmdg 2/24th Battn London Regt	19/07/1916	19/07/1916
Miscellaneous	Battalion Order In The Field By Lieut Colonel J.P.G Crosbie Cmdg 2/24th Battn London Regt	27/07/1916	27/07/1916
Heading	181st Brigade 60th Division 2/24th Battalion London Regiment (The Queens) August 1916		
War Diary	Ecurie	01/08/1916	05/08/1916
War Diary	Right 2 Sector	06/08/1916	13/08/1916
War Diary	Etrun Bde Res	13/08/1916	21/08/1916
War Diary	Right 2 Sector	21/08/1916	29/08/1916
War Diary	Bde Res Ecurie	30/08/1916	31/08/1916
Miscellaneous	Battalion Orders In The Field By Lieut Colonel J.P.G. Crosbie Cmdg 2/24 London Regiment	04/08/1916	04/08/1916
Miscellaneous	Battalion Orders In The Field By Lieut Colonel J.P.G. Crosbie Cmdg 2/24 London Regiment	12/08/1916	12/08/1916
Miscellaneous	Battalion Orders In The Field By Lieut Colonel J.P.G. Crosbie Cmdg 2/24 London Regiment	21/08/1916	21/08/1916
Miscellaneous	Raid By 2/24th London Regiments	25/08/1916	25/08/1916
Miscellaneous	Story of the Raid Made by the 2/24th Lond R. on Night of 28/29th August 1916	29/08/1916	29/08/1916
Miscellaneous	Time Table Of Raid By 2/24th Lond. R On Night Of 28/29th August 1916	29/08/1916	29/08/1916
Miscellaneous	Battalion Orders By Lieut Colonel J.P.G. Crosbie Cmmdg 2/24th Battalion London Regiment The Queen's	28/08/1916	28/08/1916
Heading	181st Brigade 60th Division 2/24th Battalion London Regiment September 1916		
War Diary	Ecurie	01/09/1916	03/09/1916
War Diary	Right 2 Sector	04/09/1916	09/09/1916
War Diary	Etrun	10/09/1916	15/09/1916
War Diary	Right 2 Subsector	16/09/1916	22/09/1916

War Diary	Ecurie	23/09/1916	28/09/1916
War Diary	Right 2 Sector	29/09/1916	30/09/1916
Miscellaneous	Battalion Orders By Lieut Col J.P.G. Crosbie Cmmdg 2/24th London Regt	03/09/1916	03/09/1916
Miscellaneous	Battalion Orders By Lieut Col J.P.G. Crosbie Cmmdg 2/24th Lon Regt	09/09/1916	09/09/1916
Miscellaneous	Battalion Orders In The Field By Lieut Colonel J.P.G. Crosbie Cmmdg 2/24th Battalion London Regiment The Queen's	16/09/1916	16/09/1916
Miscellaneous	Raid By 2/24 London Regiment	19/09/1916	19/09/1916
Miscellaneous	Battalion Orders By Lieut Colonel J.P.G. Crosbie Commdg 2/24th L.R	21/09/1916	21/09/1916
Miscellaneous	Battalion Orders By Lieut Colonel J.P.G. Crosbie Commdg 2/24th London Regt	27/09/1916	27/09/1916
Heading	181st Brigade 60th Division 2/24th Battalion London Regiment October 1916		
Heading	War Diary 2/24th Battalion London Regiment The Queens From 1st October 1916 To 31st October 1916 Vol No.1		
War Diary	Right 2 Sector	01/10/1916	04/10/1916
War Diary	Etrun	05/10/1916	09/10/1916
War Diary	Right 2 Sector	10/10/1916	16/10/1916
War Diary	Ecurie	17/10/1916	24/10/1916
War Diary	Izel-Les-Hameau	25/10/1916	25/10/1916
War Diary	Beaudricourt	26/10/1916	28/10/1916
War Diary	Barly	29/10/1916	29/10/1916
War Diary	Fienvillers	30/10/1916	31/10/1916
Miscellaneous	Battalion Orders In The Field By Lieut Colonel J.P.G. Crosbie Comdg 2/24th Battalion London Regiment	03/10/1916	03/10/1916
Miscellaneous	Battalion Orders In The Field By Lieut Colonel J.P.G. Crosbie Comdg 2/24th Battalion London Regiment The Queens	10/10/1916	10/10/1916
Miscellaneous	Battalion Orders In The Field By Lieut Colonel J.P.G. Crosbie Comdg 2/24th Battalion London Regiment The Queens	15/10/1916	15/10/1916
Operation(al) Order(s)	2/24th Battalion London Regiment Order No.14	23/10/1916	23/10/1916
Miscellaneous	2/24th Battn London Regiment March Order No.15	23/10/1916	23/10/1916
Miscellaneous	2/24th Battalion London Regiment The Queen's After Order to March Order No.15	24/10/1916	24/10/1916
Miscellaneous	2/24th Battn London Regiment March Order No.16	24/10/1916	24/10/1916
Miscellaneous	2/24th Battalion London Regiment After Order To March Order No.16	24/10/1916	24/10/1916
Miscellaneous	2/24th Battalion London Regiment After Order To March Order No.16		
Miscellaneous	2/24th Battalion London Regiment The Queen's March Order No.17	27/10/1916	27/10/1916
Miscellaneous	2/24th Battalion London Regiment The Queen's March Order No.18	28/10/1916	28/10/1916
Heading	181st Brigade 60th Division 2/24th Battalions London Regiment November 1916		
Heading	2/24th London Regiment The Queen's War Diary Volume No.1 November 1916		
War Diary	Fienvillers	01/11/1916	04/11/1916
War Diary	Mouflers Vauchelles	05/11/1916	24/11/1916
War Diary	Mouflers	25/11/1916	25/11/1916
War Diary	Vauchelles	25/11/1916	28/11/1916

War Diary	Marseilles	29/11/1916	30/11/1916
Miscellaneous	2/24th Batt London Regiment The Queen's March Order No.19	03/11/1916	03/11/1916
Miscellaneous	2/24th Battalion London Regiment The Queen's Move Order No.20		

WO 95/3032/9

60TH DIVISION
181ST INFY BDE

2-24TH BN LONDON REGT

JUN - NOV 1916

181st Brigade.

60th Division.

Battalion disembarked HAVRE 25.6.16.

2/24th BATTALION

LONDON REGIMENT (THE QUEENS)

24th JUNE to 31st JULY 1916

WAR DIARY or INTELLIGENCE SUMMARY

2/24th Batt. London Regt. The Queens.

Army Form C. 2118

Place	Date 1916	Hour	Summary of Events and Information	Remarks and references to Appendices
Warminster	JUNE 24th		Left Warminster. Wills for Southampton. Embarked for H.M.T. ARUNDEL.	E.M.S.
Le Havre	25th		Disembarked at Le Havre, France. Proceeded by route march to Rest Camp, Havre.	E.M.S.
		11.30pm	Entrained at Gare du Marchandise.	E.M.S.
St. Pol.	26th	3.40pm	Detrained at St. Pol. Proceeded by route march to Flelers into rest billets.	E.M.S.
Flelers	27th		General training in billeting area.	E.M.S.
"	28th		" " " "	E.M.S.
"	29th		" " " "	E.M.S.
"	30th		" " " "	E.M.S.
"	JULY 1st		" " " " Lt. E.R. Modderly, 2 Lt. N.C. Tennison, R.J. Bishop and Lt. Walshe and 12 O.R. attended course of instruction at Divnl. Grenade School, Hermanville. 2nd Lieut. R.B. Dewsbury & 11 O.R. transferred to 181st French Mortar Battery.	E.M.S.
"	2nd		General training in Billeting area.	E.M.S.
"	3rd		" " " " 2/Lt. S. Worssam & 20 R. attended course at Third Army Gas School. H./Col. 2/Lt. E.J. Davis & 6 O.R. attended course at M.G. School, Camiers.	E.M.S.
"	4th		General training in Billeting area.	E.M.S.
"	5th		" " " "	E.M.S.
"	6th		Moved by route march to Mareuil into rest billets.	App. I.
Mareuil	7th		To receive trenches at Ecurie, under instruction by companies - from 1/4 R. Scots and 1/4 Argyle & Sutherland Highlanders	E.M.S.

WAR DIARY or INTELLIGENCE SUMMARY

Army Form C. 2118

2/24th Batt. London Regt.
The Queens.

Place	Date 1916	Hour	Summary of Events and Information	Remarks and references to Appendices
Ecurie	July 8th		Under instruction. One N.C.O. attended Musketry Course at Camiers.	E.M.S
"	9th		2/Lt. H.L. Earl & 2 O.R. attended Sniping Course at A.C.Q.	E.M.S
"	10th		Capt. H.L. Rees & 2 O.R. attended Third Army School H. Pot. One N.C.O. attended Bombing Course at Etrun.	E.M.S
"	11th		"	E.M.S
"	12th		One man killed, one wounded.	E.M.S
In the line	13th		Relieved 1/4th Bn. Argyle & Sutherland Highlanders. Four men killed three wounded. Enemy's trench mortars active. ours retaliated effectively. Enemy exploded small mine, crater 30' broad and 20' deep. 250 steel helmets issued.	APP. 2. E.M.S
"	14th		Heavy bombardment heard on right in the early morning. Damage to trenches by shell fire very considerable. Enemy's artillery very active. Ours replied effectively to French Mortars. Capt. H.F.T. Magnus reported from 1/24th Bn. L.R. 100 steel helmets issued.	E.M.S
"	15th		Our T.M. destroyed enemy sniping-post. One of our sniping non-coms killed & party wounded. 117 steel helmets issued. Lt. E.V. Knight & 2/Lt. J. McKillop reported from Reserve Unit.	E.M.S
"	16th		Relieved by 2/22nd Bn. L.R. and moved into rest billets at Etrun.	E.M.S
Etrun	17th		In rest billets. 3 O.R. on Pigeon Post course at 17th Corps H.Q.	E.M.S
"	18th		"	E.M.S
"	19th		2/Lt. E. Horssam & 9 O.R. attended course in Lewis Gunnery. Capts. Lazic & H. Magnus 2/Lt. J. McKillop & 4 O.R. attended Anti-gas course at Frevin Capelle.	E.M.S
In the line	20th		Relieved 1/22nd Bn. L.R. by 8.15 a.m. Enemy front line damaged by our Krupp shells. Reinforcing draft of 70 O.R. received from 15th Batt. Lon. Regt.	APP. 3. E.M.S

WAR DIARY
or
INTELLIGENCE SUMMARY
(Erase heading not required.)

2/24th Batt London Regt Army Form C. 2118
The Queens

Instructions regarding War Diaries and Intelligence Summaries are contained in F.S. Regs., Part II. and the Staff Manual respectively. Title Pages will be prepared in manuscript.

Place	Date 1916	Hour	Summary of Events and Information	Remarks and references to Appendices
In the Line	JULY 21st		Considerable damage observed to Enemy front & support line trenches by our T. Mortars.	2 N. S
"	22nd		" " " " " " doing very little damage.	2 N. S
"	23rd		H.E. shrapnel fired at our front lines, doing very little damage.	"
"	24th		Bombing and rifle grenade raid made by enemy doing no damage. This was dispersed effectively. Considerable damage observed on Enemy lines through T.Ms & Artillery.	2 N. S
"	25th		Enemy much quieter in retaliating to our T.Ms which were very busy. Several of our bombs falling into enemy's trenches.	2 N. S
"	26th		Enemy T.M. emplacement believed destroyed completely by our French Howitzer, Stokes & Field gun fire.	2 N. S
"	27th		Situation normal.	2 N. S
"	28th		Battalion relieved by 2/2nd Bn. Lon. Regt. Moved to Ecurie. One Zeppelin brought down felt observer located enemy.	APP. B. 2 N. S
Ecurie	29th	9pm	Our batteries of artillery bombarding the enemies front & support lines on our line of advance. Zeppelin sighted at 9pm flying from NE to NW on approaching our line it turned & then back in NE direction.	2 N. S
"	"	"	Under instruction Lieuts C. Raynor, I.N.O. and E. O.R. attending Divis Bombing School ETRUN Lieut C. Mobberley, 2nd Lieut N.C. Dennison & 4 NCOs attending	2 N. S
"	"	"	Cadet Gas School. PLEVIN CAPELLE.	
"	30th		Three wounded. One acct of accident.	2 N. S
"	31st		Our artillery active during day. Enemy retaliating with Trench mortars. Some Gas shell exploded near ECURIE CHURCH at 8.15 pm. One enemy aeroplane flew over ECURIE during evening.	2 N. S

APP. I.

SECRET.   No.11.

2/24th Battn. London Regt., March Order No.1.

Ref.
LENS 11 1/100,000.   Headquarters.
                                      2/24th Battn. London Regt.
                                      5th July 1916.

1. MOVE.

   The Battalion, including Transport (Echelon "A" & "B"), will be formed up in column of route at 6 p.m. on the CHELERS - TINCQUES ROAD head of column at "A" Cos. Headquarters, and move to MAROEUIL.

2. ROUTE.

   Via TINCQUES - ARRAS, ST POL ROAD and CROSS-ROADS, 100 yards W of E of ETRUN.

3. ADVANCE PARTY.

   Advance Party will leave billets at 1.30 p.m. and report to Town Major MAROEUIL at 4 p.m. Officer i/c. to meet Battalion at cross-roads 100 yards W of E of ETRUN to act as guide into billets.

4. CERTIFICATES.

   O.C. Companies will render certificates on departure and arrival in billets as laid down in Battalion Standing Orders for Billets, and Battalion Orders No.7, Para 5, dated 4th July 1916.

5. Acknowledge.

                                      Captain & Adjutant.
                                      2/24th Battalion London Regiment,
                                          The Queen's.

Copies to.

1. File.
2. 154th Infantry Brigade.
3. "A" Co.
4. "B" Co.
5. "C" Co.
6. "D" Co.
7. O.C. Transport.
8. Quartermaster.
9. 181st Infantry Brigade.

APP. 2:

BATTALION ORDERS IN THE FIELD

      by

Lieut. Colonel J.P.G.Crosbie,
Cmmdg. 2/24th Battn.London Regt. The Queen's.

                            12th July 1916.

<u>RELIEF</u>   The Battalion will relieve the 1/7th Argyll & Sutherland Highlanders tomorrow, as follows.-

1. Lewis Guns, Signallers, Snipers, Bombers, will relieve in advance as detailed.

2. Companies will relieve as follows.-

   "C" & "D" Cos. will relieve "C" & "D" Cos. 1/7th A.&.S.Highlanders and will take over their sectors during forenoon as per instructions issued by O.C. 1/7th A.&.S.Highlanders. "C" Co. will hold left sector, "D" Co. centre sector.

3. "A" Co. will relieve "A" Co. 1/7th A.&.S.Highlanders and take over right sector.

4. "B" Co. will relieve "D" Co. 1/7th A.&.S.Highlanders and will be in support.

5. <u>GUIDES.</u>- 4 Guides from 1/7th A.&.S.Highlanders will report to O.C. "A" & "B" Cos. at 2 p.m.

6. O.C. "A" & "B" Cos. will not leave their Coy. H.Q. at ECURIE and SUNKEN ROAD till they have handed over to their opposite numbers in 2/22nd London Regiment, and reported relief to Battn. H.Q. at ECURIE.

7. All Companies will report time of completion of relief to Battn.H.Q. POSTE LILLE.

- 2 -

8. ATTACHMENT.- 1 Officer and 2 N.C.O's. per Company will be attached to the Battalion for instructional purposes from the 1/7th A.&.S. Highlanders.

9. WORKING PARTIES.- O.C. "B" Co. will detail 1 N.C.O and 20 men to report to a R.E.Officer at the MINOTAUR DUMP at 9 p.m. 14th July 1916. All other available men in Support Company will be made up into parties of 7 each under an N.C.O. ready to start work at 9.30 p.m. Further details will be issued later.

                   (Sgd) E.M.GREEFF.
                    Captain & Adjutant.
          2/24th Battn. London Regiment,
                    The Queen's.

AFTER ORDER

    Messages concerning reliefs must never be sent by telephone.

APP. 3.

BATTALION ORDERS IN THE FIELD

by

Lieut.Colonel J.P.G.Crosbie,
Cmmdg. 2/24th Battalion London Regiment.

19th July 1916.

RELIEF.- The Battalion will relieve the 2/22nd. Battn.London Regt., tomorrow, 20th July 1916, as follows.-

1. Lewis Guns, Signallers, Snipers will relieve in advance as detailed. Snipers will parade outside Brigade Headquarters at 1 p.m. Bombers will proceed with their Companies. Battalion Bombers with the first platoon of "C" Co.

2. Companies will relieve as follows in Sub-sector, Right 2.

   "D" Co. will be left Company.
   "A" Co. will be centre Company.
   "B" Co. will be right Company.
   "C" Co. will be in support.

   Companies will leave ETRUN in the following order

   "B", "A", "D", "C".

   proceeding at 10 minutes interval between platoons. First platoon of "B" Co. to pass ANZIN CHURCH at 3 p.m. and move up AVENUE FANTOME, remaining Companies will follow in succession and move up ANNIVERSAIRE AVENUE.

GUIDES.- 4 Guides per Company from the 2/22nd. Battn.London Regt., will be at ANZIN CHURCH at 2.50 p.m.

- 2 -

<u>TRENCH STORES.</u>- The R.S.M. and C.S.Ms. will leave billets at 2 p.m. and report to their opposite numbers and take over trench stores.

N.B. Copy of Trench Stores taken over by O.C. Companies must be sent to Battalion Headquarters as soon as possible after taking over.

<u>WORKING PARTY.</u>- "A", "B" & "D" Cos. will each detail 1 N.C.O. and 9 men and "C" Co. will detail 1 Officer, 1 N.C.O. and 11 men to report to LILLE POST at 9.30 p.m. Each man to carry a pick and shovel. The Officer will report to the Adjutant at 9 p.m. for instructions.

O.C. Companies will report relief complete to Battalion Headquarters.

<u>BILLETS.</u>- O.C. Companies will render a certificate to the Adjutant before leaving that all billets are clear and have been left clean.

(Signed) E.M. GREEFF.
Captain & Adjutant,
2/24th Battalion London Regiment,
The Queen's.

App. 4

BATTALION ORDERS

by

Lieut.Colonel J.P.G.Crosbie,
Cmmdg. 2/24th Battalion London Regiment.

27th July 1916.

1. **Relief.** The Battalion will be relieved by the 2/22nd London Regt. as follows, and will be in Brigade Reserve at "C" position on the 28.7.16.

2. "A" Co. will be relieved by "C" Co. 2/22nd and will move to ABRI MOUTON and relieve "D" Co. 2/21st.

   "B" Co. will be relieved by "A" Co. 2/22nd and will move to ABRI CENTRALE and relieve "A" Co. 2/21st.

   "C" Co. will be relieved by "D" Co. 2/22nd and will move to ECURIE VILLAGE and relieve "B" Co. 2/21st.

   "D" Co. will be relieved by "B" Co. 2/22nd and will move to SUNKEN ROAD and relieve "C" Co. 2/21st.

3. **Guides.** O.C.Companies will each send one guide per platoon for 2/22nd to be at ANZIN CHURCH at 12.50 p.m. Guides from 2/21st will be at Coy. H.Q. at about 2.30 p.m.

4. On arrival in "C" position O.C. "B" Co. will be under the orders of O.C. 2/21st.
   O.C. "A" Co. will be under orders of O.C. 2/22nd.
   O.C. "D" Co. will be under orders of O.C. 2/22nd.
   i.e. for all matters relating to tactics and working parties; not for interior economy and discipline.

4. Continued.
   The usual trench returns will be rendered to the Adjutant by these Companies with the exception of situation, intelligence and work done.

5. Trench Stores. List of trench stores on charge of Coys. must reach Bn.H.Q. by 10 a.m.

6. Companies will report relief complete by runner to Bn.H.Q. TUNIS and POST LILLE.

        (Sgd) E.M.GREEFF.
          Captain & Adjutant.
   2/24th Battalion London Regiment.

181st Brigade.
60th Division.

2/24th BATTALION

LONDON REGIMENT (THE QUEENS)

AUGUST 1916.

WAR DIARY or INTELLIGENCE SUMMARY

Army Form C. 2118

181/60 Vol III 2/24 Lond. R.

Place	Date	Hour	Summary of Events and Information	Remarks and references to Appendices
Ecurie	1/8/16.		Course of Instruction: One NCO and 4 O.R. Trench Mortar Battery Course. Lijny de Hocke. Throughout the day there was Artillery activity on both sides.	S.N.S. S.N.S.
"	2/8/16.		Course of Instruction. Three O.R. Lifting course at ACQ. Artillery activity throughout day. Fourteen aeroplanes flown over enemy lines seen throughout one day. Very fine, according to our lines MANZIN CHURCH. Hostile aircraft observed over EGURIE.	S.N.S.
"	3/8/16.		Artillery and Trench mortar activity on both sides throughout day. Hostile observation balloons up. Aircraft over ECURIE taken off by gunfire.	S.N.S.
"	4/8/16.		2/Lt A. Evans wounded.	S.N.S.
"	4/8/16.		Very quiet today any slight wide artillery trench mortars.	S.N.S. APP A
"	"	6.35pm.	Fine. two killed (all attached) seen infor of Therus for short time.	
"	5/8/16.		Artillery trench mortar activity on both sides. Things of slight moment on outer ring in course ring of H. 6, 8 sight. One of the two khaki coloured airplanes drew down by machine gun fire on our right. one ripped claim one hit. The Battalion relieved the 1/12 Battn London Regt. the relief was complete by 3.40pm.	S.N.S.
Right 2 Sector	6/8/16.		Slight artillery trench mortar activity during the day. On 10.15pm our boutdarse a color in enemy line opposite Brigade front to our left. Two enemy aeroplanes open damage. anything. Two observation balloons up throughout day. On enemy again one hit. Course of Instruction. 9 O.R. Brigade Bombing School, ETRUN.	S.N.S. S.N.S.
"	7/8/16.		Casualties: Two wounded. Working party working in hostile trades defences by Lifte Grenades. There was general activity on both sides throughout the day with little mortar activity. fire carried and on our right at 9.30pm, one hostile aeroplane driven off by flick. Enemies sent exp cracked by one of ours duyes. The pigeons flew from enemy lines in N. direction.	S.N.S.

WAR DIARY
or
INTELLIGENCE SUMMARY
(Erase heading not required.)

Army Form C. 2118

Instructions regarding War Diaries and Intelligence Summaries are contained in F.S. Regs., Part II. and the Staff Manual respectively. Title Pages will be prepared in manuscript.

Place	Date	Hour	Summary of Events and Information	Remarks and references to Appendices
Rights 2 Sector.	8/8/16.	6.50pm	The day was quieter. There was an exchange of artillery & trench mortar fire during the day. Another ambulance convoy was going from easterly direction into Ypres. One of our aeroplanes flew over our lines in direction of Ypres and dropped bomb which appeared to do considerable damage. Another hostile aeroplane has been noted at A.16.C.8.8. Enemy instruction. Capt. J.R. Figg & two O.R. 2nd Army Infantry School came to Chateau.	SWS
"	9/8/16.		Caesarfio. One wounded. Considerable activity with trench mortars & artillery. Two wire entanglements hostile Sap at A.16.C.8.8. Hostile working party seen in support line which our artillery dispersed. Two pigeons flew from our lines to hostile aeroplane & were seen two of our aeroplanes found to land & hostile aeroplane travelled near & hovering over German motor cyclists travelled along road in horizon travelling from Yelouin South Easterly Direction.	SWS
"	"			
"	"			
"	10/9/16.		Inneschis. Two wounded. Wire especially to be seen. Rabit Coy. active together with certain amount of trench mortar fire. Rifle grenades fired with good results. Machine gun fire during night from Booten 91. A22. C.35.40. hostile trench mortar between Vista at A. 22. C.35. 60. Heard aeroplane activity during day. Patrol went out shortly of position A.23.C.25.48. but was forced to withdraw under rifle gunfire.	SWS
"	11/8/16		The day was quieter. Our artillery became active between 4.10 am 4.10 am. There was also a certain amount of Trench Mortar activity. Rifle grenades were fired with good results. Enemy machine guns were active firing chiefly at our dumps. At 12.45pm four	SWS

1875 Wt. W593/825 1,000,000 4/15   J.B.C. & A.   A.D.S.S./Forms/C.2118.

WAR DIARY or INTELLIGENCE SUMMARY

Army Form C. 2118

Place	Date	Hour	Summary of Events and Information	Remarks and references to Appendices
Nijh 12 sche.	11/5/16		While flying along German lines from South to halt. One hostile observation balloon was up in rear of Thelus but was moved at night. No hostile aircraft was seen during the day.	EWS
	12/5/16		The artillery was quiet during the forenoon, becoming active during the afternoon evening. Our artillery bombarded craters $\frac{5 \times}{1}$ & $\frac{7 \times}{1}$ a & $\frac{7 \times}{1}$ a and caused considerable damage to its forward eps/ posts. 9 which were blown down level with the ground. Some enemy 5.9 guns were used at 2.45 pm but did no damage. A red light went up from the German line 9/Km artillery opened on our trenches. Four red Xxxx & Then bombardment ceased. Carrier 2.O.R. "Communication between Infantry & Aircraft" Rendezvous at SAPS. (Cancelled) One O.R. wounded.	EWS
	13/5/16		The Battalion was relieved in the front line by the 1/22nd Loncolns Regt & proceeded to their Billets in ETRUN where general training was carried out until 21st inst. Courses during this period 13th Anti-Gas 2nd Lieut J Mekarongo & 4 O R 13th Brigade Bombing School 1st Lieut A B Ashford & 10 O R 14th Physical Training 2nd Lieut Dutt & 4 O R 15th Consolidation of Craters 2nd Lieut H Brownwich & 1st Lieut La Fond & O R 15th Lullingphone J.O.R. 3 O R 17th Ziping 3 O R 19th Loopsfone 7 O R	as before

WAR DIARY
or
INTELLIGENCE SUMMARY
(Erase heading not required.)

Army Form C. 2118

Place	Date	Hour	Summary of Events and Information	Remarks and references to Appendices
ETRUN Bû-de-Ang	13/21 Aug 1916		Courses Corner 18th Consolidation of Centre, Lieut C.V. Knight, 2 Lieut E.T. Davis & O.R. 20th Brigade Bombing School 2 Lieut D.S. Cunningham + 8 O.R. 20th Telephone 2 O.R. 21st Interrogatyons in trenches by 17 inst. 1 O.R. Accidentally injured	J.D.

Army Form C. 2118

WAR DIARY
or
INTELLIGENCE SUMMARY
(Erase heading not required.)

Instructions regarding War Diaries and Intelligence Summaries are contained in F. S. Regs., Part II. and the Staff Manual respectively. Title Pages will be prepared in manuscript.

Place	Date	Hour	Summary of Events and Information	Remarks and references to Appendices
Ryld 2 siche	21/8/16		Casualties 2 O.R. Our artillery was only moderately active during the day. During the night they fired some shells apparently at the enemy dumps & reserve trenches. Our Stokes guns were active during the day. Our aircraft were active during the day. One hostile aeroplane was seen over our lines at 4.15 p.m. The Batt. relieved the 2/22nd Batt. London Regt. was complete at 7.0 p.m. Course of Instruction. Lewis gun course at Touquet. L/Cpl. Mobberley. Course on Trappe Control duties 3 O.R.	GHS
"	22/8/16		Artillery fired intermittently during the day chiefly on the German front line. Enemy Trench Mortars were active during day. Enemy flew in pairs of BONNA TRENCH SUTHERLAND AVENUE. Enemy artillery fires heavy shrapnel over on our right sub sector. Two enemy observation balloons were up in rear of Thelus. Course of Instruction in Telephones 2 O.R. at Chivres.	GHS
"	23/8/16		Our artillery fired intermittently during the day. Enemy Trench Mortars were pretty quiet. Enemy snipers were very quiet, very probably to bad light. Casualties 5 O.R.	GHS
"	24/5/16		Our artillery only slightly active during day except at 7.5 p.m. when they bombarded the enemy front line @ 11.0 p.m. an intense bombardment by our guns started on our left. Enemy artillery did not seem to retaliate much. And at 11.15 pm to 6.12 pm they sent over a good many Trench Mortars & whizz bangs. However along SPOONER AVENUE	GHS

1875 Wt. W593/826 1,000,000 4/15 J.B.C. & A. A.D.S.S./Forms/C. 2118.

WAR DIARY or INTELLIGENCE SUMMARY

Army Form C. 2118

(Erase heading not required.)

Place	Date	Hour	Summary of Events and Information	Remarks and references to Appendices
Auchy 2 sect.	24/8/16		& unnamed trench in sa of GRAND COURRETTE at F.16 & F.17. Enemy observation balloons were up during the day one NE & another SE of exatic XIV. Casualties 2 O.R.	EMC
"	25/3/16		Bombardments under Divisional arrangements took place at 4.0pm & 4.30pm - 4.40pm Enemy Trench Mortars were active during day. One of Stokes Gun was hit by a shell. SUTHERLAND AVENUE was damaged in 3 places by Trench Mortars. The BOTTOM TRENCH at A.16.C.43.62 was badly damaged by 5.9 shells. At 2.0pm an enemy aeroplane was observed over our reserve trenches. It was heavily shelled & one of the shells burst just in front of it. The aeroplane dropped & came down in very uneven spirals some three to four hundred feet but managed to escape.	SMC

WAR DIARY
or
INTELLIGENCE SUMMARY

(Erase heading not required.)

Army Form C. 2118

Place	Date	Hour	Summary of Events and Information	Remarks and references to Appendices
Right > Sector	26/6/16		Our artillery active throughout the day. Fuzes being brought up to our lines from enemy lines. Attempts to find this by enemy were abortive. Casualties. 2 O.R. Wounded.	S.W.S.
	27/6/16		Course of instruction 2nd Lieut Bennison and 9 O.R. Bombing. 2 O.R. Anti- Gas.	
	28/6/16		Our Trench Mortars active. Artillery less so. Casualty 1 O.R. Killed.	
			Our Artillery and Trench Mortars active. Enemy retaliation feeble. Casualty 1 O.R. Wounded.	
	29/6/16		Raid made upon two enemy craters and adjacent trenches. Remainder of day was quiet. Batt. relieved in Right Sector by 2/5th Lincoln Regiment and relieved 2/1st & 2/2nd Jordan Regiment in Brigade Reserve. Casualty 1 O.R. accidentally wounded.	see App. "I" see App "II"
Bde Res FEURIE	30/6/16		Situation quiet. Weather very wet.	
			F⁵ Weather improving	

Appendix A

BATTALION ORDERS IN THE FIELD

by

Lieut. Colonel J.P.G.Crosbie,

Cmdg. 2/24th London Regiment.

4th August 1916.

1. **RELIEF.-** The Battalion will relieve 2/22nd London Regt. in RIGHT II on 5th August 1916, as follows.-

2. Signallers, Bombers, Lewis Gunners and Snipers will relieve in advance as detailed. The relieve will commence at noon. Companies will relieve as follows.-

"A" Co. will relieve "C" Co. 2/22nd, and will be in the centre.

"B" Co. will relieve "D" Co. 2/22nd and will be in support.

O.C. "B" Co. will arrange with O.C. "A" Co. 2/22nd. that ABRI CENTRALE is relieved by 3.30 p.m.

"C" Co. will relieve "A" Co. 2/22nd and will be on the right.

O.C. "C" Co. will arrange with O.C. "B"Co. 2/22nd. that BOURIE is not left ungarrisoned any time during the relieve. 1 Guide per Platoon from 2/22nd, for "C" Co. will be at BOURIE Company Headquarters at 12 noon.

"D" Co. will relieve "B" Co. 2/22nd and will be on the left.

3. **TRENCH STORES.**

O.C.Companies will send a list of trench stores handed over, to Battalion Headquarters, TUNIS. An Officer will be left behind from each Company to attend to this. O.C.Companies will arrange to send their Company Sergeant Majors on ahead to take over trench stores, in the forward area.

4. **REPORTS.-** O.C.Companies will report relieve complete by runner to Battalion Headquarters, LILLE POST. Any casualties sustained during the relieve will be reported immediately to Battalion Headquarters, by runner.

IN THE FIELD.
4th August 1916.

Captain & Adjutant,
2/24th London Regiment.

APPENDIX B

BATTALION ORDERS IN THE FIELD

by

Lieut. Colonel J.P.C.Crosbie,
Cmmdg. 2/24th Battalion London Regiment.

12th August 1916.

1. **Relief.** The Battalion will be relieved in Right II by the 2/22nd London Regt on the 13th August as follows, and proceed to rest billets at ETRUN.

2. Signallers, Lewis Gunners, Snipers and Bombers will be relieved in advance as detailed.

3. Companies will be relieved as follows. The relief will commence at about 2.30 p.m.

    "A" Co. 2/22nd will relieve "C" Co. 2/24th.
    "B" Co.   "   "   "   "A" Co.
    "D" Co.   "   "   "   "D" Co.
    "C" Co.   "   "   "   "B" Co.

4. **Trench Stores.** O.C.Coys will send a list of trench stores handed over to their opposite numbers, duly signed by both O.C.Coys.

5. **Control Posts.** O.C. "B" Co. will arrange to send guards on in advance to take over Control Posts from 2/21st by noon. The R.S.M. will issue necessary details to N.C.Os. i/c. of guards.

6. **Reports.** O.C.Coys. will report relief complete to Battn.H.Q. LILLE POSTE by phone in the following code.
"FOR FURTHER PARTICULARS SEE SMALL HAND BILLS".

7. **Halts.** On no account will platoons halt in ANZIN.

8. **Billets.** C.Q.M.S's. have been instructed to meet their Coys. and conduct them to billets. Company runners must be at Battn. H.Q. 30 minutes after arrival of Companies in billets.

   "D" Co. will be the Company in waiting and must be ready to move if so ordered in 30 minutes.

9. **Handing Over.** In handing over O.C.Coys. will pay special attention to point out to their opposite numbers what work they have been doing re maintenance of trenches and all details about guards and sentries.

Acknowledge.

(Sgd) E.M.GREEFF.
Captain & Adjutant,
2/24th Battalion London Regiment.

Issued by Orderly as follows,-

Copy No.1. O.C. "A" Co.
    2.   "   "B" "
    3.   "   "C" "
    4.   "   "D" "
    5. 2/22nd London Regt.
    6. File.

APPENDIX C

BATTALION ORDERS IN THE FIELD FOR MONDAY 21-8-16.

by

Lieut. Colonel J.P.C. Crosbie,
Cmdg. 2/24th Battalion London Regiment,
The Queen's.

1. **RELIEF.**— The Battalion will relieve the 2/22nd Battalion London Regiment, in Right II on the 21st August 1916, as follows.—

   Signallers, Bombers, Lewis Gunners and Snipers will relieve in advance as detailed. Companies will commence relieving at 2.15 p.m. in the following order at the following times. Companies will move from ETRUN to ANZIN, by platoons, at 5 minutes interval, the leading platoon of "B" Co. to reach ANZIN COMMUNICATION TRENCH by 3 p.m.

   Companies will proceed to the trenches in the following order.

   "B" Co.
   "A" Co.
   "D" Co.
   "C" Co.

   DISPOSITIONS. Dispositions will be as follows.—

   "B" Co. will relieve "A" Co. 2/22nd. Lond.Regt, and will be on the right.

   "A" Co. will relieve "B" Co. 2/22nd. London Regt. and will be in the centre.

   "D" Co. will relieve "D" Co. 2/22nd. London Regt. and will be on the left.

   "C" Co. will relieve "C" Co. 2/22nd. London Regt. and will be in support.

   ROUTE. Platoons must not halt in ANZIN. On no account will platoons, or any parties of platoons, proceed across the open from ANZIN to MADAGASCAR.

2. **TRENCH STORES.**— O.C.Companies will detail 1 Officer per Company and their C.S.M. to proceed to the trenches during the morning and take over trench stores.

3. **REPORTS.**— On completion of relief, O.C.Companies will report, by wire in the following code.
   "WE ARE ALL IN IT".

4. **RUNNERS.**— O.C.Companies must send runners to Battalion Headquarters as soon as possible after taking over.

5. **CASUALTIES.**— Any casualties sustained during the relief will be reported in clear, by runner, to Battalion Headquarters.

6. **RATIONS.**— Times for sending ration parties to the dumps will be notified later.

Captain & Adjutant,
2/24th Battalion London Regiment,
The Queen's.

In The Field.
20-8-16.

O.C. 2/24 Bn L.R.   APPENDIX D

SECRET   Copy No 10

RAID BY
2/24th LONDON REGIMENT
------oOo------

Reference Maps :- NEUVILLE ST VAAST 1/5000
                  and TRENCH MAPS

To take place on AUGUST 29th 1916

Under 2/Lieut H.L.EARLE and 2/Lieut H.C.BILTON (2nd in command)

OBJECT - To obtain identifications & cause damage to enemy.

    JUMPING OFF POINT   A.22.b.22.39 (Crater XII)

        OBJECTIVE   A.22.b.18.55 (Crater XIXa and XIX)

    POINT OF RETURN   A.22.b.19.29 (Crater XIV)

The party will consist of FOUR GROUPS as under :-

    "A" Group   Rear blocking party, under 2/Lieut H.C.BILTON of 1 N.C.O. and 6 men. Duty of this Group will be to prevent any of the enemy discovered in the Crater from retiring on their own front line.

    "B" Group   Left blocking party 1 N.C.O. & 3 men. Duty of this Group will be to cover main raiding party.

    "C" Group   Right blocking party, 1 N.C.O. &3 men. Duty of this Group will be to cover main raiding party.

    "D" Group   Under 2/LIEUT H.L.EARLE, 1 N.C.O. and 11 men; two of these men to look after ladder and tape, which will be taken into Crater from Sapheads. Duty of this Group, to drive through Crater XIXᵃ then XIX Crater, capture any enemy in either and destroy any works found.

------oOo------oOo------

1. **METHOD OF CARRYING OUT RAID**

    The Crater will be rushed at a time which will be known as ZERO.
    At - 25 minutes the party will leave Crater XIV and proceed to jumping off point (Crater XII), from which point the groups will crawl out to their respective positions in following order :-
    A Group   B Group   C Group   D Group
    All Groups will be in position by ZERO, and the raiding party will be lined out on the near lip, ready to advance. "A" Group will crawl into the crater under cover from the German lines and seize any enemy retreating before "D" Group's advance.

2. **PRIMARY OBJECT OF RAID** is to secure a prisoner, in any case the party will hold the Craters for 10 minutes and gain as much information of the enemy's positions as possible. They will also endeavour to destroy with bombs any works they may find, and bring back any articles of clothing etc. which would be useful as means to identification.

(Signal

3. SIGNAL FOR WITHDRAWAL at 10 minutes will be showers of GREEN rockets from Right Companies advanced and Main Headquarters. 2/LIEUT H.L.EARLE will superintend the withdrawal of all parties and remain on the near lip of Crater XIX^a with the 8 Battalion bombers ("B" and "C" parties) to cover retirement.
2/LIEUT H.C.BILTON will lead the retirement, but on reaching Crater XII (the jumping off point), will stay until all the parties have passed him, he will be responsible for counting them.
The retirement will be assisted by two tape men, the first remaining on the near lip of Crater XIX^a with rope ladder, the second remaining laying by the tape between Craters XIX^a and XII, this man will also check numbers. On arrival at point of return (Crater XIV) the party will be again checked by an officer.
A shower of RED, WHITE, RED, WHITE, RED, WHITE rockets will be fired from right companies Headquarters when the party has returned complete.
The whole raiding party will remain in Crater XIV until they receive instructions to do otherwise from Battalion Headquarters.

✕ This will be the Signal for cease fire.

4. The men of the raiding party will wear, steel helmets and service dress with puttees, but will NOT wear equipment. All means of identification will be removed, including private letters etc, marking on inside of clothing etc. will be obliterated. Faces will be blacked, and both shoulder straps will be bound with white tape.

5. ARMS CARRIED BY RAIDING PARTY

   "A" Group   3 bayonet men
                    3 bombers
                    N.C.O. armed with revolver.

   "B" Group   N.C.O. armed with revolver, and bombs.
                    2 bayonet men
                    1 bomber.

   "C" Group   as for "B" Group

   "D" Group   N.C.O. armed with revolver
                    4 bombers
                    5 bayonet men
                    1 ladder & 1 tape man

   Each man will carry one MILL'S BOMB in left pocket of tunic.
   Every bomber will carry a LIFE-PRESERVER.
   Every bayonet man will carry 9 rounds in magazine, and 1 in chamber of rifle, with an additional 10 rounds in right hand pocket of tunic.
   BOMBERS - each man will carry 10 bombs, selected men will carry "P" bombs.

6. All ranks will be warned that in the event of their being captured by the enemy, they will on no account give the name of their Regiment, Brigade or Division, but should state their number, name and initials.
Special identity discs will be issued.
No identification marks, such as cockades, number plates etc. must be taken from any prisoner as souvenirs.

(Accommodation

-3-

7. **ACCOMMODATION OF RAIDING PARTY.** the party will be garrisoned in Crater XV prior to the Raid.

8. A final reconnaissance will be carried out on the evening of the 28th inst.

9. There will be no movement in the BONNAL from - 30 minutes, until "Cease Fire" and down traffic will make way for all up traffic. in communication trenches

10. **MEDICAL AID POSTS** a special post will be established in Crater XIV½ and casualties will be evacuated direct from there to Aid Post near LILLE BARRICADE, the route to which will be picqueted.

11. **STORES TO BE CARRIED BY MEN**

      4   Revolvers.
      2   Wire traverser matresses.
  110   Bombs.
      4   Wire Cutters
           Tape
   60   Yards of Strong Cord (each man carrying 6 yards)
   17   Life Preservers.
    6   Pairs of Hedging gloves.
           Rope ladder
      4   Electric torches.
           Special identity discs.

12. The wire round Crater XIX^a will be cut on afternoon of 28th by T.M's. At + 3 minutes the artillery will bombard the enemy's trench mortar positions and support line, until "Cease Fire" signal is sent up. Feint bombardments will be carried out by T.M's

13. An advanced telephone station will be established in Crater XIV.

14. The watches of all concerned in the operation will be sent to Battalion Headquarters to be syncronised at 5 p.m. on the 28th August

15. There will be no password or code used in these operations.

16. Company Commanders will ensure that all Sentry Posts are warned of the operations on hand by - 40 minutes.

17. A hot meal will be served to the raiding party on return.

18. ZERO time will be notified later.

19. Acknowledge.

John Croshé

Lieut-Colonel
Cmdg. 2/24th London R.

25-8-16

STORY OF THE RAID MADE BY
the 2/24th LOND R.
on night of 28/29th August
1916

----o----   ----o----

Reference RAID carried out by Battalion under my command last night 28/29th August on Craters XIX and XIX^a. This RAID was planned with a view to obtaining an identification, Very lights had been seen several nights previously fired from inside the Craters and on early morning 27th a man was seen to be moving round the rear edge, these facts made it appear possible that the Crater was held and certainly patrolled.

The raiding party succeeded in surrounding the Crater as arranged, without being discovered. An enemy machine gun near the LILLE ROAD opened fire in the direction of the party, but no casualties occurred.

The party entered the Craters at ZERO as arranged, but found no enemy or enemy work of any sort.

The old mine shaft is still visible in North Wall of XIX Crater, it could not be discovered in the time how far this shaft ran, possibly well behind enemy front line, Crater XIX is not connected to the enemy front line by any Sap, nor is there any sign of the Crater being held on the North lip by a sentry group. An old trench runs out from the enemy line towards Crater XIX as shown in aeroplane photographs, but ends 20 yards from the Crater and is strongly wired; this trench is not held by the enemy. Bombs were thrown by the party into this trench and wire in front of enemy front line, no reply was received. From observation from these Craters the enemy front line appears to be weakly held, few lights were sent up from this line. The party returned at ≠ 10 minutes as arranged. The Artillery support appeared good and enemy T.M. were in most cases silenced, the enemy appeared to answer only with T.M's and field guns.

No casualties were incurred.

(sgd) J.CROSBIE
Lieut-Colonel
29-8-16   Cmdg. 2/24th London R.

TIME TABLE
of
RAID BY 2/24th LOND. R. ON NIGHT OF
28/29th August 1916

1.45 a.m.	Raiding party leave position of assembly.
2. 9 a.m.	Raiding party in position.
	<u>A Group</u> on Western inside lip of Crater XIX
	<u>B Group</u> on Southern lip inside Crater XIXa
	<u>C Group</u> on Northern lip inside Crater XIX
	<u>D Group</u> on Western lip of Crater XIXa
2.10 a.m.- 2.20 a.m.	D Group sweeps through Crater XIXa and XIX, but find no trace of the enemy. Eastern lips examined and hostile front line bombed.
2.13 a.m.	Artillery and T.M. fire opens.
2.15 a.m.	Stokes T.M's cease fire.
2.20 a.m.	Recall Signal fired. Stokes T.M's open on second objective.
2.21 a.m.	First white guiding rocket fired.
2.24 a.m.	Stokes T.M's Cease fire.
2.30 a.m.	2" T.M's cease fire
2.32 a.m.	2/Lt. EARLE and 11 O.R. reported in
2.35 a.m.	2/Lt. BILTON and 8 O.R. reported in, 8 still missing.
2.44 a.m.	Cease fire signals, all guns cease except Howitzer Battery and 1 18 pr. Battery. Firing of Recall rockets ceased.
2.55 a.m.	Howitzer and 18pr Batteries cease fire.
3.10 a.m.	All in except 5 men, one man slightly wounded by comrades bayonet.
3.50 a.m.	All in except one man.
3.50 a.m.- 6. 0 a.m.	Search parties out, missing man returns at 6 a.m.

xxxxxxxxxxxxxxxxxxxxxxxxxxxx

APPENDIX E

In The Field.   28-8-16.

BATTALION ORDERS

by
Lieut. Colonel J.P.G. Crosbie,
Cmmdg. 2/24th Battalion London Regiment,
The Queen's.

---

1. **Relief.**   The Battalion will be relieved by the 2/22nd London Regt. on 28-8-16 as follows and will move into Brigade Reserve at "C" position.

2. Signallers, Bombers, Lewis Gunners, Snipers, will be relieved in advance as detailed.

3. "A" Co will be relieved by "B" Co. 2/22nd and will move to SUNKEN ROAD, and relieve "C" Co. 2/21st.

   "B" Co will be relieved by "C" Co. 2/22nd and will move to ECURIE and relieve "B" Co. 2/21st.

   "C" Co will be relieved by "A" Co. 2/22nd and will move to ABRI CENTRALE and relieve "A" Co. 2/21st.

   "D" Co will be relieved by "D" Co. 2/22nd and will move to ABRI MOUTON and will relieve "D" Co. 2/21st.

4. **Route.**   Companies will move to their positions by the following communication trenches.-

   "A" Co. via MINATAUR AVENUE.
   "B" Co. via FANTOME   "
   "C" Co.) via LABYRINTHE, MADAGASGAR Avenue, VILLAGE STREET,
   "D" Co.)   ROCKLINCOURT AVENUE.

5. Companies at SUNKEN ROAD, ABRI MOUTON, will be under orders of O.C. Right II. Company at ABRI CENTRALE will be under orders of O.C. Right I.

6. **Maintenance of Trenches.-**   Before leaving Right II, O.C.Companies will point out to their opposite numbers what work has been and is being undertaken. On Arrival in "C" position, O.C.Coys. will pay particular attention to take over all work concerning maintenance of communication trenches and will see that work is commenced the following day.

7. **Trench Stores.**   Greater care must be exercised in the handing over of Trench Stores than has heretofore been taken. Any stores that are damaged and need repair must be sent to Battalion Headquarters and struck off the list of Trench Stores. List of stores duly signed by an Officer of the incoming and outgoing Company to be sent to Battn.H.Q. as soon as possible after handing over.

8. **Reports.**   O.C.Companies will report relief complete to Battn.H.Q. in the following code, by wire, "SHELL OUT".

9. **Runners.**   Runners between Company and Battn.H.Q. in "C" position will be arranged by the intercommunication Officer.

10. Acknowledge.

(Sgd) E.M.GREEFF.
Captain & Adjutant,
28-8-16.   2/24th Battalion London Regiment.

181st Brigade.
60th Division.

2/24th BATTALION

LONDON REGIMENT.

SEPTEMBER 1916.

Army Form C. 2118

2/24 London
Vol 4
181/60

WAR DIARY
or
INTELLIGENCE SUMMARY
(Erase heading not required.)

Place	Date	Hour	Summary of Events and Information	Remarks and references to Appendices
Ecurie	1/9/16		Course of Instruction. 2nd Lt Nickport and 3 O.R. Lewis gunners an A.C.G. During the day enemy was heavily shelling with 5.9" 50% of which were duds. 5 Hostile observation balloons aloft.	E.M.S.
"	2/9/16		Our artillery very active carrying out "Lifting" fire. One hostile aeroplane shewn over ECURIE at 11 A.M. Two hostile observation balloons aloft. Stationary rea light seen over THELUS.	E.M.S.
"	3/9/16		Course of Instruction. 2nd Lt Ashford. 1 NCO & 8 O.R. Bombing. Our artillery very active at STRUN. Our artillery very active on rear lines and area on NEUVILLE ST. VAAST and THELUS. Two hostile observation balloons aloft. Our aircraft moderately active.	E.M.S.
Reghts 2 Section	4/9/16	5/30 pm	The Battalion relieved the 2/22nd Bat London Regt. Enemy's artillery moderately active. Our artillery and trench mortars retaliated. Enemy aeroplane seen over lines in Sector XIX and two over trenches on life up. Enemy very active and found anything touching post has been erected over life up.	Do appendix A. E.M.S.
"	5/9/16		Casualties 1 wounded. Enemy artillery bombarded our trenches. Trench mortars and T.M.s very active. Having M.G's carried out some programme of firing. A patrol went out to Craters XIX and found it unoccupied. Hostile bombing barrage commenced on Chaplin 2.16 A.M. Hostile aeroplane seen flying over the near lip of Crater. One hostile aeroplane flying over the lines.	E.M.S.

Army Form C. 2118

WAR DIARY
or
INTELLIGENCE SUMMARY
(Erase heading not required.)

Instructions regarding War Diaries and Intelligence Summaries are contained in F.S. Regs., Part II. and the Staff Manual respectively. Title Pages will be prepared in manuscript.

Place	Date	Hour	Summary of Events and Information	Remarks and references to Appendices
Rights B/2	6/9/16		Enemy's wire very thick, but the day were cutting it. One S.P. Lee dropped in centre where enemy was cutting [illegible] forward gun. Enemy bombardment on our left today. Two Fokkers attacked our Artillery Patrol went out from the company sectors are necessary repairs in progress.	ENS
"	7/9/16		Extracted M.G.S. guns and one O.C. wounded. Major J. Gordon one O.R. accidentally wounded. Enemy rather active throughout the day on part of enemy mortars broken. Enemy M.G. plaintain active. 2nd Hampshires returned. Much indirect MG fire kept up by our line from Fokkers were active. Fokker works. Batteries & Brigade HQ shelled but no casualties. One Fokker brought down in flames on Western side.	ENS
"	8/9/16		Both artillery and Trench mortars very active. One member of Weston Riflles formed into Funy Patrol. Two Fokkers mechanical trouble landed against enemy. Two Fokkers observation following our working party & were disposed with Lewis Gunners.	ENS
"	9/9/16		Artillery and Enemy aerial observation active as integral during the day Snipers Lieut A.22. a 95. 6. and Battery find on west Lye Snipers. Top 33 engaged by enemy T.M. Lengincey observation post camera on A.22 C.M. 55 and A.22 L.38.42. One Fokker Aeroplane seen at 3.30 pm. And aerograph survey.	ENS

1875 Wt. W593/826 1,000,000 4/15 J.B.C. & A. A.D.S.S./Forms/C. 2118.

WAR DIARY or INTELLIGENCE SUMMARY

Army Form C. 2118

Place	Date	Hour	Summary of Events and Information	Remarks and references to Appendices
Etrun	10/9/16		The Battalion was relieved by the 9/22nd Batt London Regt. Course of Instruction. Irish Women and 7.O.R. Bombing Course at Etrun 2nd Lieut Bond and 4.O.R. Auto Rifle Course. 3 O.R. Lewis Course etc.	See appendix "D" E.N.S
"	11/9/16		Battalion employed in General training.	E.N.S
"	12/9/16		Course of Instruction. 2nd Lieuts Y.G. Hitching & O.R. Exploration of Orders. 7.O. Lieuton. General Training.	E.N.S
"	13/9/16		Battalion employed on General Training. Course of Instruction. 3 O.R. Sniping Course at HQ.	E.N.S
"	14/9/16		Battalion employed on General Training	E.N.S
"	15/9/16		Battalion employed on General Training	E.N.S
Night 2. Lebecho	16/9/16	6/30 p.m	My Battalion was relieved the 9/2nd Batt London Regt. The Battn moved at 6.30 p.m. Lewis Guns deployed a hostile working party being very actively . This was fairly active during remainder of day	See appendix "D" E.N.S

Army Form C. 2118

WAR DIARY
or
INTELLIGENCE SUMMARY
(Erase heading not required.)

Instructions regarding War Diaries and Intelligence Summaries are contained in F.S. Regs., Part II. and the Staff Manual respectively. Title Pages will be prepared in manuscript.

Place	Date	Hour	Summary of Events and Information	Remarks and references to Appendices
Dugout 62 Ishrector	17/9/16		Tours of Instruction. Bombed 9 O.R. Bombing force at Etreux profited. Bond and 9 O.R. mortars employed in wire cutting. Field artillery and trench mortars fairly successful. Third Artillery and 18 pounders enemies retaliation weak. Every night inspecting Japanese enemies parties were active, our own night patrols encountered parascope sp'ln'rs at A16. C.70.45.	E.H.S.
"	18/9/16		Gun artillery trench mortars & machine guns very active throughout day. Stokes gun dispersed a hostile working party in trench at A16. C.70.50. Enemy retaliation very much. Patrols on owning thought Weather very hot.	E.H.S.
"	19/9/16		Casualties O.R. 2 wounded. 1 on duty. General Activity on our side without incident. Trench mortars rifle grenades & enemy trench mortars played tolerably good thing on OLD MILL. Enemy trench mortars rather strong on BARBO, raising kept up by wire laying parties behind THELUS and Road. Klaxon warning of bent lights. Enemy transport heard from Enemy on expansion of Thelus. Patrols were out listening throughout several Bocks observed along of THELUS going along road to BOIS CARRE at 9 pm.	E.H.S.
"	20/9/16		Gun artillery very active throughout Today. twice ripping 6. Heavies fired on OLD MILL THELUS. Our machine guns active on gaps in hostile line. Enemy retaliated rather more actively. Transport heard in direction of THELUS. Activity observed THELUS on part of enemy who marched along road in pairs towards BOIS CARRE.	E.H.S.

WAR DIARY or INTELLIGENCE SUMMARY

Army Form C. 2118

(Erase heading not required.)

Place	Date	Hour	Summary of Events and Information	Remarks and references to Appendices
Right 2 Sector	21/9/16		Casualties 3 O.R. wounded. Enemy of Laventie. 2 O.R. French mortar borne. Raid arrived at enemy's position. Effective was not reached on account of enemy activity. Await other French now considerably active. Enemy activity in wiring and round THELUS to party from breastwork, wiring and round THELUS to small group of Enemy seen party of about 30 used seen on BOIS CARRÉ ROAD. Two hostile aeroplanes over our lines.	G.W.S. See appendix 5
"	22/9/16		Another small raid on enemy position on the party being again driven off by hostile opposition. Casualties 2nd Lieut. J.C. Bilton and 2 O.R. wounded. 2nd O.R. wounded. Enemy artillery active throughout the day. Enemy by artillery & trench mortar active at 12 noon and proceeded towards Red Cross wagon seen to leave THELUS at by our guns and 9.30 am southerly direction. Two hostile aeroplanes observed driven off by our guns and gas. and the Battalion was relieved by 2/22nd Batt. L.R. at 4.30 pm.	As appendix 6 G.W.S. As appendix 6
ECURIE.	23/9/16		Our artillery and trench mortars active. Two hostile observation balloons aloft and two hostile aeroplanes observed.	G.W.S.
"	24/9/16		Course of Instruction. 2nd Lieut. Powys 1-9 O.R. Brig. at Bombing School. Having fired on Bosche on THELUS establishing walls and masonry. Enemy aircraft active through out the day. One machine cruising above a gun returned safely. Enemy mortar active, there being very little retaliation to our French mortar artillery fire.	G.W.S.

Place	Date	Hour	Summary of Events and Information	Remarks and references to Appendices
ECURIE	25/9/16		Our Artillery continued its activity on enemy line & also on THELUS during evening. Some damage also done on "HAY STACKS" securing fine strong point today. Our Aircraft very active. One machine being brought down by enemy fire about A.15. Two two seaters and a Scout. Two obtained at 1.55 p.m. One hostile aeroplane seen and two observation balloons to our front.	E.N.S.
"	26/9/16	11.45 AM	Light artillery active also trench mortars but only moderately. No provision wagon seen to leave THELUS at 1.55 p.m. Our Aircraft made numerous reconnaissance raids. One machine enemy forced to descend inside party. Fair flown left wing. Hostile machines seen at 11.15 am & again at 11.45 pm.	E.N.S.
"	27/9/16		Our Artillery fired on enemy lines "Haystacks" and on OLONIE N OF THELUS. Some of THELUS being bombarded. ECURIE and LILLE ROAD in vicinity of ROCLINCOURT shelled at 7.30 p.m. A Zepplin was lighted up at A.21 & A.40.85. Our Aero Gun unable to fire. Zepplin seen observation balloons of enemy optically no draw enemy artillery. Enemy observation balloons of THELUS as described bearing the day. 4 Star lights sent up during the day.	E.N.S.
"	28/9/16		Moderate activity on part of our Artillery. Heavy firing again on our Stokes & Mrs ! Stokes trench mortars not active. Left of our front enemy active also on Mrs ! Stokes & Trench mortar set up by enemy. High two green Very lights sent up by enemy. Bath also relieved the 1/2nd Batt London Regt at 4.5 pm. Practically the Batt also relieved to day.	E.N.S.
"		4.5 pm		
Right 2 Sector	30/9/16		Artillery much quieter. No new scheme. Hostile working party at A.6. C.73. 80 dispersed with Stokes gun fire. Raid made on our left. Numerous Verey lights 50 red/dark & very green. Stokes gun fire. Raid made on our left forward. Patrols were out along from our front reply enemy two active from. During the night but have nothing fresh to report. No enemy snipers working patrols were seen.	E.K.S.

WAR DIARY or INTELLIGENCE SUMMARY

Army Form C. 2118

Place	Date	Hour	Summary of Events and Information	Remarks and references to Appendices
Right B Sector	30/9/16		Heavy against our trench and works to N. of Old Mill Trench. Much intersection during day. Two hostile aeroplanes seen at 11.30 a.m. and 12.15 p.m. Our aircraft flying very low over enemy lines & attacked one of the wire machine guns. Enemy any work, any wires retaliated to our fire.	E M S

Appendix A

Battalion Orders   In the Field
by
Lieut Col J.R.L. Leslie commdg.
2/24th London Regt
3/9/16

---

1. **Relief** - The Batta will relieve 2/22nd LR in Right II on 4th Sept 1916 as follows:-

2. **Time** - The relief will commence at 2pm

3. **Specialists**. ie Signallers, Bombers, Lewis Gunners, Snipers. will relieve in advance as detailed.

4. **Dispositions**:-
   A Coy will relieve B Coy 2/22nd in the Centre
        B Coy 2/22nd will move to ECURIE.
   B Coy will relieve C Coy 2/22nd on the Right
        C Coy 2/22nd will move to ABRI MOUTON
   C Coy will relieve D Coy 2/22nd on the Outposts
        D Coy 2/22nd will move to SUNKEN RD
   D Coy will relieve A Coy 2/22nd on the Left
        A Coy 2/22nd will move to ABRI CENTRALE.

5. **Route** - Coys will move to their Subsectors as detailed -

6 *Trench Stores* - OC Coys will send on in advance their CSM. to take over Trench Stores. - OC Coys will send a list of Trench Stores handed over to Batt H.Q. Tunis. - an Officer will be left behind to attend to this.-

7 *Reports* - OC Coys will report relief complete by wire in the following code -
"Thats all right as long as I know.
Any casualties sustained during the relief will be reported by runner immediately to Batt H.Q.

8° *Acknowledge*

(signed) E.M. GREEFF

Capt & Adyt
2/24th Lon Regt

Appendix "B"

Battalion Orders in the Field
by
Lieut Colonel J.P.G. Leslie
Commdg 2/24th Lon Regt

9/9/16

1. **Relief** - The Batt. will be relieved in Right II by the 2/22nd on the 10th Sept as follows and proceed to rest billets in ETRUN. -

2. **Signallers**, Lewis Gunners, Snipers and Bombers will be relieved in advance as detailed. -

3. **Coys** will be relieved as follows the relief will commence at about 3.30pm

    A Coy 2/22nd will relieve B Coy 2/24th
    B   "   "   D   "
    C   "   "   A   "
    D   "   "   C   "

4. **Trench Stores** - OC Coys will send a list of trench stores handed over to their opposite numbers duly signed by both OC Coys.

5. **Control Post** - OC D Coy will arrange to send guard on in advance to take over Control Post

from 2/21st by noon – The R.S.M will issue necessary details to N.C.O.'s i/c of guards –

6 – Reports – O.C. Coys will report relief complete to Batt H.Q. LILLE POSTE by phone in the following code
"LOOK WHO'S HERE"

7 – Halts – On no account will platoons halt in ANZIN, or proceed across the open in small parties from MADAGASCAR to ANZIN

8 – Billets – C.Q.M.S's have been instructed to meet their Coys and conduct them to billets – Coy runners must be at Batt H.Q 30 minutes after arrival of Coy in billets – D Coy will be the Coy in waiting and must be ready to move if so ordered in 30 minutes

9 – Handing over – In handing over O.C Coys will pay special attention to point out to their opposite numbers what work they have been doing re maintenance of trenches and all details about guards and sentries –

10 Acknowledge

(signed) E M GREEFF
Capt: Odyt
9/9/16   2/22nd Lon Regt

Appendix "C"

BATTALION ORDERS IN THE FIELD FOR SATURDAY 18-9-15.

by

Lieut. Colonel J. W. Frowhig, commdg
2/24th Battalion London Regiment
"The Queen's"

1. **RELIEF.** The Battalion will relieve the 2/22nd Battalion London Regiment in Right 71 on the 18th September 1915, as follows :-

    Machine Guns, Bombers, Lewis Gunners and Snipers will relieve in advance as detailed. Companies will commence relieving at 2.15 pm in the following order at the following times. Companies will move from ETRUN to ACHIN by platoons at 5 minutes interval - the leading platoon of "B" Coy. to reach ACHIN COMMUNICATION TRENCH by 3 pm.

    Companies will proceed to the trenches in the following order :-

    "B" Coy.
    "A" Coy.
    "C" Coy.
    "D" Coy.

    DISPOSITIONS. - Dispositions will be as follows :-

    "B" Coy will relieve "A" Coy 2/22nd London Regt and will be on the right.

    "A" Coy will relieve "C" Coy 2/22nd London Regt and will be in the centre.

    "C" Coy will relieve "D" Coy 2/22nd London Regt and will be on the left.

    "D" Coy will relieve "B" Coy 2/22nd London Regt and will be in support.

    ROUTE. Platoons must not halt in ACHIN. On no account will platoons, or parties of platoons, proceed across the open from ACHIN to MAZINGARBE.

2. **TRENCH STORES.** - O.C.Companies will detail 1 officer per Company and their N.C.O. to proceed to the trenches during the morning and take over trench stores.

3. **REPORTS.** - On completion of relief O.C. Companies will report by wire in the following code :-
    "This and That".

4. **RUNNERS.** - O.C.Companies must send runners to Battalion Headquarters as soon as possible after taking over.

5. **CASUALTIES.** - Any casualties sustained during the relief will be reported in clear by runner to Battalion Headquarters.

6. **RATIONS.** - Times for sending rations parties to the dumps will be notified later.

7. ADDRESSES.

H.DAVIDGE,
Lieut & Adjutant,
2/24th Battalion London Regiment.

18.9.15.

SECRET.   *Appendix D*   Copy No......6....

RAID BY
2/24 London Regiment.

To take place on night of 20/21st September/16.
under Sec.Lieuts. H.C.BILTON and H.T.BRODERICK.

Reference Maps NEUVILLE ST.VAAST 1/5,000 and Trench Maps.

...   .

OBJECTS. Cause damage to the enemy and obtain an identification.

	Right Party.	Left Party.
Jumping-off points	Sap 30B	Crater 34.
Objectives	A.22.a.88.94.	A.16.c.70.40.
Points of Return.	Same as Jumping-off points.	

The party will consist of four groups as under:-

(a) <u>Right Raiding Group</u> under Sec.Lieut. BRODERICK -
                                 4 N.C.Os. and 21 men.
(b) <u>Right Connecting Group</u> under Lieut. C.V.KNIGHT -
                                 1 N.C.O. and 11 men.
(c) <u>Left Raiding Group</u> under Sec.Lieut. H.C.BILTON -
                                 4 N.C.Os. and 21 men.
(d) <u>Left Connecting Group</u> under Sec.Lieut. C.WORSSAM -
                                 1 N.C.O. and 11 men.

1. METHOD OF CARRYING OUT RAID.

The German front line will be penetrated at ZERO at A.22.a.88.94 and A.16.c.70.40 and trench in immediate vicinity raided during a period of 30 minutes. The connecting groups will drop men in pairs between the jumping off points and objectives. During the raid any prisoners or booty obtained will be passed back to the point of jumping off and return by the connecting groups. No identification marks such as cockades, number plates, etc. must be taken from any prisoners captured.

2. Primary Objects of Raid.

To discover in what manner and in what strength the German front line is held at these points and the condition of the trenches: to destroy any Machine Gun or Trench Mortar emplacements; and to endeavour to obtain an identification by capturing a prisoner or any other means available.

3. Withdrawal.

At plus 30 minutes, the raiding parties will withdraw and retire to jumping off points, being assisted by the connecting groups. One Very light will be fired per minute from ECURIE Defences to ensure these parties taking the right direction, commencing at plus 35 minutes. Os.C. raiding parties will remain on enemy's parapet until their last man has left the enemy trench. They will then acquaint the O.C. their respective connecting group who will be responsible for retirement of his party.

4. The men of both raiding and connecting groups *cotton bandoliers* will wear steel helmets and service dress with puttees, but will not wear equipment. All means of identification will be removed, including private letters, etc. Marking on inside of clothing will be obliterated, both shoulder straps will be bound with white tape and Officers will wear a band of white tape on each arm. All bayonets will be dulled. Special identity discs will be issued.

5. Arms Carried by Raiding Parties.

A & C Groups. All N.C.Os. will carry revolvers, 13 men with rifles, and bayonets, 8 bombers.

- 2 -

      B & D (Connecting) Groups - 1 N.C.O. with revolver, 11 men rifles and bayonets.

Each man will carry one Mills Bomb in left jacket pocket. Every bayonet man will carry 9 rounds in magazine and 1 in chamber of rifle, with an additional 10 rounds in right jacket pocket. Each bomber will carry 10 Mills Bombs and one life preserver. Selected men will carry "P" Bombs. All rifles must be examined to see safety catches are applied before the parties go out.

6. All ranks will be warned that, in the event of their being captured by the enemy, they will on no account give the name of their regiment, Brigade or Division, but should state their number, name and initials only.

7. A final reconnaissance will be carried out on the evening of 20th inst.

8. There will be no movement in the BONNAL from -30 minutes until normal conditions are resumed. This time will be notified from Bn. H.Q. by the code message - "GET BREAKFAST READY".
In Communication Trenches, "DOWN" traffic will make way for all "UP" traffic during this period.

9. Medical Aid Post will be the usual Battalion Aid Post, but two stretcher parties will be in attendance at the mine tunnels in the BONNAL at top of MORAY AVENUE on right, and the BONNAL near the Sap leading into 34 Crater on the left, respectively.

10. Stores carried by the men :-

        10 Revolvers.
        2 Wire traverser mattresses.
     208 Mills Bombs.
        6 Wire Cutters.
      60 Yards strong cord.
      16 Life Preservers.
        4 Pairs Hedging Gloves.
        4 Electric torches.
          Special identity discs.
        4 Sandbags full of torn paper.

11. The wire at both objectives will be cut on the afternoon of 20th inst. by Trench Mortars.

12. An artillery barrage on enemy's support line will be arranged by Right Group Commander but will not be used unless called for from Bn. Headquarters, who will also notify the time to "Cease Fire".
Signal for Barrage to open - Red-Green-Red-Green rockets.
Signal for "Cease Fire" will be the usual 3 red rockets.

13. Watches of all concerned will be sent to Bn. H.Q. to be synchronised at 5 p.m. on 20th inst.

14. There will be no pass-word or code used in these operations.

15. Company Commanders will ensure that all sentry posts are warned of the operations on hand by - 50 minutes.

16. A hot meal will be served to raiding and connecting groups on return.

17. All ranks are warned that these operations must be carried out with the greatest possible silence. The bayonet only is to be used, except in the case of occupied German dugouts being discovered.

18. ZERO will be notified later.

19. ACKNOWLEDGE.

20. All reference to these operations will be referred to as "WHAT NOT".

                                                John Crosbie
                                                     Lieut. Col.
19.9.16.   Cmdg. 2/24 London Regt.

Appendix "C"

In the Field   21/9/16

Battalion Orders
by
Lieut Colonel G.P.L. Crabbie
commdg 2/24th L.R.

───────────────

1. Relief - The Battn will be relieved by the 2/22nd
   L.R. on 22/9/16 as follows & will move into
   Bde Reserve at C position.

2. Signallers. Bombing. Lewis Gunners, Snipers
   will be relieved in advance as detailed

3. A Coy will be relieved by C Coy 2/22nd and
   will move to ABRI MOUTON and relieve A Coy
   2/21st.

   B Coy will be relieved by A Coy 2/22nd and will
   move to SUNKEN ROAD and relieve D Coy 2/21st

   C Coy will be relieved by B Coy 2/22nd and will
   move to ABRI CENTRALE and relieve C Coy 2/21st.

   D Coy will be relieved by D Coy 2/22nd and will
   move to ECURIE and relieve B Coy 2/21st

4 - Coys will move to their position by the usual communication trenches.

5 - Coys at SUNKEN ROAD - ABRI MOUTON will be under orders of O.C Right II - Coy at ABRI CENTRALE will be under order of O.C Right I

6 - Maintenance of trenches - before leaving Right II - O.C Coys will point out to their opposite numbers what work has been done and is being undertaken - On arrival in C position O.C Coys will pay particular attention to take over all work concerning maintenance of communication trenches and will see that work is commenced the following day.

7. Trench stores. - Lists of stores duly signed by an Officer of the incoming & outgoing Coy to be sent to Battn H.Q. as soon as possible after handing over. - Unsigned list of Trench Stores are to be sent to Batt H.Q. as early as possible tomorrow morning.

8 _Reports_ - OC Coys. will report relief complete to Batt H.Q. in the following code by wire - "HOBSON'S CHOICE"

9 _Runners_ - Runners between Coys & Batt H.Q. in C position will be arranged by the intercommunication Officer.

10 _Rest_ - OC Coys will make every endeavour to see that men obtain as much rest as possible -

11 - _Acknowledge_ -

(signed) E. N. GREEFE

21/9/16   Capt. Adjt
                       2/24 L R

Appendix F
In the Field

Battalion Orders
by
Lieut Col E P L Cobie commdg
2/8th London Regt
27/9/16.

1. <u>Relief</u> - The Battn will relieve the 2/22nd LR
   in Right II on 28th Sept 1916 as follows -

2. <u>Time</u> The relief will commence at 1.15 pm
   A Coy will not commence till 1.45 pm.

3. <u>Specialists</u> ie Signallers. Bombers, Lewis
   Gunners & Snipers will relieve in advance
   as detailed -

4. <u>Dispositions</u> -
   A Coy will relieve D Coy 2/22nd in the
   Supports who will then move to SUNKEN RD
   B Coy will relieve B Coy 2/22nd on the Left
   who will then proceed to ECURIE
   C Coy will relieve A Coy 2/22nd on the Right
   who will then proceed to ABRI CENTRALE
   D Coy will relieve C Coy 2/22nd in the Centre
   who will then proceed to ABRI MOUTON. -

5. **French Stores** – OC Coys will send on in advance their 2nd in Command & WSM to take over French Stores – OC Coys will send a list of French Stores handed over to Batt H.Q. Lunis. An Officer will be left behind to attend to this.

6. **Reports** – OC Coys will report relief complete by wire in the following code.
 "Take me in the Gate !!"
Any casualties sustained during relief will be reported immediately to Batt H.Q. by runner.

7. **Route** – Usual route will be taken – OC Coys will see that Platoons do not straggle – several times during the last relief this was very noticeable.

8. **Acknowledge**

(signed) E. M. GREEFF
Capt / Adjt
2/2nd Lon Regt

28/9/16

181st Brigade.

6 0th Division.

2/24th BATTALION

LONDON REGIMENT

OCTOBER 1916.

Secret.

18/6 Vol 5

War Diary.
2/24th Battalion London Regiment.
The Queens

From :- 1st October 1916.
To :- 31st October 1916
Vol. No 1.   Copy No 5.

John Crosbie
Lieut Col

WAR DIARY of 1/1st LONDON REGT
INTELLIGENCE SUMMARY

(Erase heading not required.)

Army Form C. 2118

Instructions regarding War Diaries and Intelligence Summaries are contained in F.S. Regs, Part II. and the Staff Manual respectively. Title Pages will be prepared in manuscript.

Place	Date	Hour	Summary of Events and Information	Remarks and references to Appendices
Hebuterne Schl.	1/10/16		Course of Instruction 2 Lieut. Wilkinson and 9 O.R. Brigade Bombing School. Enemy has been today damaged by our artillery and has sunk as fire. Enemy aircraft engaged enemy balloon. Enemy guns open on retaliation but only Vickers working party at F.16. C.40. No prisoners. Enemy shows nothing today. Rob'd. others. We observe movement and observation balloon.	C.M.E.
"	2/10/16		Today an active day. Some enemy activity in neighbourhood. No retaliation. Activity in neighbourhood of the L.15 continues. Aeroplane was very light. One of the enemy's approaching to accompany other enemy flying round and watching for our guns opened.	C.M.E.
"	3/10/16		Very foggy till 11 a.m. No active today. Our artillery opened fire into enemy registered on enemy trenches preparations for raid. Enemy activity with trench mortars, whizz-bangs to heavy. Hy. Hows. bombs into Hill. Our own batteries engaged the enemy machine guns. Aeroplane activity. Hy. Howitzers at 5.55 pm shells dropped and enemy's own light trench mortars S.E. direction. No opera. Howitzers now adapt during the day.	C.M.E.
"	4/10/16		Very dull wet. Work not necessary hy. Hows. artillery & trench mortars. Enemy retaliated by enemy scraping vicinity of trench. Regt. Battalion was relieved by the 1/2nd Bn. London Regt. Course Instruction. 3 O.R. Lewis gun course. The Battalion carried out General Training.	C.M.E. see appx I
ETRUN	5/10/16		Course of Instruction.	C.M.E.
"	6/10/16		Cpl. Shire and 2 others + 6 O.R. Inspection of Gases. Battalion carried out General Training.	C.M.E.

Army Form C. 2118

WAR DIARY
or
INTELLIGENCE SUMMARY

2/24th Batt Lon Regt

(Erase heading not required.)

Place	Date	Hour	Summary of Events and Information	Remarks and references to Appendices
ETRUN	31/8/16		The Battalion continued General Training and Instruction. 3 O.R. employed forming.	M.S
"	1/9/16		Lieut J. Hughes and Major J. Legat & 4 O.R. Anti Gas Course. 2nd Lieut Aubrey & 9 O.R. Signalling School. The Battalion continued General Training.	M.S
"	2/9/16		General Instruction. 2/Lt Macpatt R. Shepherd J.J. & 6 O.R. Reconnaissance of Ground. Battalion endured training was inspected by Corps Commander.	M.S see Appendix "A"
Right 2 Sector Lubeau	3/9/16		General Instruction. Lieut Menlove & 2 O.R. Anti Gas Course. Instruction. The Battalion relieved the 4/7 Batt Zealand Regt. Sometime of picture Henri Camp trenches and Regt Headquarters.Everything went off without a hitch. Battalion on arrival of our ap everywhere knowing every inch of the ground. Relief was complete at 6.40pm	M.S
"	4/9/16		Received orders on the back of our Brigade that for any demonstration of aggression on our Brigade a reply would be given. Enemy were quite during the day. Enemy were rather active. Our artillery fired bursts of shrapnel 4 mins by our artillery. Shots at 15 secs. Lasting 1- 5 mins approximately. Our artillery enfiladed the trench in range 7x18 Aux 2.9 Arm. Enemy replied very sharply at our infantry.	M.S
"	5/9/16		General Situation - Trench mortars mostly mainly active. There's old rifle works used, on the IX & side emergency 350 yards south right of HELLS WOOD. Enemy retaliation weak. They reply to trench m. by using artillery of several kinds. Field battery medium trench mortar & minute werfers 2 official reported 2 copies of Box body working at reported to 2nd RA. Lewis guns fired 500 rounds open on our Box SABRE or southrail of enemy also caused.	M.S

Army Form C. 2118

WAR DIARY
or
INTELLIGENCE SUMMARY

(Erase heading not required.)

2/24th Batt. Lon Regt

Place	Date	Hour	Summary of Events and Information	Remarks and references to Appendices
Regtl 3rd Sector	13/10/16		Received from Report lines shelled with artillery and Trench Mortars. A.16. C.20.25 bombards action. Enemy fired on track B.1. Road avoid Village Road 6" howitzers. Enemy heavy trench Mortars fired on junction into GREEN AV BONNAR Avenue. L.S.O.S also firing rockets tracking into two red lights. Enemy lids quantities of rifle grenades on our line between N 30-35. Activity numerous patrols & our THELUS officers patrols were out.	S.M.S.
"	14/10/16		Tour of Instruction. Capt N. Lewitt & B.K. Lear. 2 OR. 1st Army Schol. Considerable activity shown by enemy artillery, but reduced engaging scattered following up our artillery fire, but there was nothing at all felt. This also again at BONN. (Watlohl) Enemy retaliated and T.M.s again heard. This falling along Trench on inner N in GREEN AV. Numerous coloured rockets and lights by enemy during night. Again along D 3.0.9 at 11.1 but being covered there was nothing abnormal. Large Minie observed at 6.30pm in direction of ARRAS.	S.M.S.
"	15/10/16		Tour of Instruction. 2nd Lt. J. Profitt on OR. Bombing Schol. Enemy showed increased activity along enemy's parapet on 5.15am enemy observed carrying large quantity of this artillery activity during day observed parapets being repaired. Enemy were active about Salton W. During day GREEN AV. Enemy heavy M.Gs active. Both Salton W and Rifle of T.M.fire. Enemy during afternoon no trenches were damaged by enemy artillery. The fire. Enemy during night no hostile action. Any M.G. attached specks no enemy seen. No hostile patrol were working along Trench. Enemy light railway working.	S.M.S.
"	16/10/16	4.30.pm	Tour of Instruction. 1st Lt. N. Hynes. 4 OR. Lewis Gun Course. Enemy again fired ropes along enemy parapet. Artillery activity active. Enemy observation Balloon found successful activity that moderately active. Enemy exploded 2 mins red smoke signal send in R.B.15 GREEN Before artillery. No tow explored Salton N. Enemy found Crew on right in our N Trench on 16 M p.15. Battalion relieved by 2/22 Bn London Regt. The evening.	T.M.S. see Appendix B

1875   Wt. W593/826   1,000,000   4/15   J.B.C. & A.   A.D.S.S./Forms/C. 2118.

WAR DIARY
or
INTELLIGENCE SUMMARY

of 12th Batt. Lon. Regt.

Army Form C. 2118

(Erase heading not required.)

Place	Date	Hour	Summary of Events and Information	Remarks and references to Appendices
ECURIE	17/10/16		Artillery and Trench mortars throughout the day. There were sounds being fired into Roclincourt village and occasionally into our trenches. Enemy machine gun was very active. Enemy machines flying very low.	M.S.
"	18/10/16		Enemy ECURIE during the morning, but although heard not observed. Our machines as then enemy trench mortars moderately active during afternoon, manner of "Minnie" being much used. Two of the trenches were working along our lines from "Cache Ro" at 12.15 pm	M.S.
"	19/10/16		Our artillery carried on ordinary damage to enemy's wire during shelling. Reds. Light pieces of gun turned on Roclincourt Keep occurring not relieved during ? wiring. Enemy fired LITTLE BROMPTON and ECURIE during the evening VILLAGE of being shelled with H.E. Shrapnel at 9.45 am. Bombarded by counter-making observation in accurate to aircraft activity below few days.	M.S.
"	20/10/16		Increased activity on part of our artillery trench mortars. There being shelled something were vice. Enemy aimed more rifle grenade today, ECURIE being again being of H.E. (5.9 + 4.2) during about of enemy searched for trench grips out artillery being fired from LABYRINTH REDOUBT. Our weather being clearer our aircraft was bombarded by these were being active. One enemy machine crew at 9.30 pm. and looked observation balloons were shot.	M.S.
"	21/10/16		Calm day. Two G.R. Kind of artillery active firing on our and enemy burning evening from a support trench. Also work a machine gun in vicinity of some trenches. Our trench mortars give some retaliatory fire was greater today. Sundry and indirect firing scheme. Enemy artillery fire was greater today. They fired on ECURIE, MAROEUIL and on the MINATEUR DUMP. One very two aeroplanes over balloon line. Our aircraft made it uncomfortable under of palace. One hostile machine driven off by gunfire. Seen at 12.30 pm. which was driven off by gunfire.	S.S.

WAR DIARY or INTELLIGENCE SUMMARY

Army Form C. 2118

1/5th Batt. Lon. Regt.

Place	Date	Hour	Summary of Events and Information	Remarks and references to Appendices
EC 0 R 15	22/10/16		Our Artillery fired Smoke projectors 52½ Bombs active on our right front in support. But leaving field on enemy's trench on receiving orders. Enemy in front appeared no artillery fire. At 4.45 p.m. an air patrol halted to a piece over the Ridge being five Hun machine to shell enemy in full swing on enemy machine firing and won down again and enemy stopped until except for damaged fifteen on BETHUNE Rd. Another hostile reactive error fires of hypouridirements around Hound.	SMS
"	23/10/16		Normal activity on our front with artillery general mortar effort of the Canadian wounded Rifles where our ramp knew preparatory to taking over the sector.	SMS
"	24/10/16	7A.M.	The Battalion was relieved by the 4th Canadian mounted Rifles and marched to MARŒUIL. Rest d'etat at 2.30 p.m. started off marched to IZEL-LES-HAMEAU.	SMS see appendix 5
IZEL-LES-HAMEAU	25/10/16		Marched to BEAUDRICOURT.	SMS
BEAUDRICOURT	26/10/16		{ Carried out General Training.	SMS see appendix 6
"	27/10/16			SMS
"	28/10/16		Marched to BARLY	SMS see appendix 7
BARLY	29/10/16		Marched to FIENVILLERS.	SMS see appendix 8

Army Form C. 2118

WAR DIARY
or
INTELLIGENCE SUMMARY
24th Batt. Lon. Regt.
(Erase heading not required.)

Instructions regarding War Diaries and Intelligence Summaries are contained in F.S. Regs., Part II. and the Staff Manual respectively. Title Pages will be prepared in manuscript.

Place	Date	Hour	Summary of Events and Information	Remarks and references to Appendices
FIENVILLERS	30/10/16		Battalion carried out General Training.	SM.5
"	31/10/16		Battalion carried out General Training.	SM.5

John Crosbie.
Lt. Colonel.
Commdg 1/24th Batt Lon Regt.
The Queens

1875 Wt. W593/826 1,000,000 4/15 J.B.C. & A. A.D.S.S./Forms/C. 2118.

Order No 11. Appendix I

Battalion Orders in the Field   3/10/16

By

Lieut - Colonel J.P.G.Crosbie Commgd,
                    2/24th Battalion London Regiment.

---

1. RELIEF. - The Battalion will be relieved by the 2/22nd London Regiment in Right II on the 4th October 1916 and will proceed to rest billets in ETRUN.

2. Signallers, Lewis Gunners, Snipers and Bombers will relieve in advance as detailed.

3. Companies will relieve as follows - relief to commence at about 3.30 pm.

    "A" Coy 2/22nd will relieve "A" Coy 2/24th.
    "B"   do.   "D"   do.
    "C"   do.   "C"   do.
    "D"   do.   "B"   do.

4. TRENCH STORES. - O.C.Coys will send to Batt H.Q. list of trench stores handed over to their opposite numbers duly signed by both O.C.Coys.

5. CONTROL POSTS. - O.C. "A" Coy will arrange to send guards on in advance to take over Control Posts from 2/21st by noon - The R.S.M. will issue necessary details to N.C.O's i/c of guards

6. REPORTS. - O.C.Coys will report relief complete to Batt H.Q. MILLE POST by phone in the following code -
    "SO I STOPPED AND I LOOKED AND I LEFT".

7. HALTS.- On no account will platoons halt in ANZIN or proceed across the open in small parties from MADAGASCAR to ANZIN - This order has always been improperly carried out - instances have always occurred of Platoons halting in ANZIN - Infringements of this order will be severely dealt with - O.C. Coys will see that this order is read out to Platoons

8. BILLETS. - C.Q.M.S have been instructed to meet their Coys and conduct them to billets. - Coy runners must be at Batt H.Q. 30 minutes after arrival of Coy in billets - A Coy will be the Coy in waiting and must be ready to move if so ordered in 30 minutes.

9. HANDING OVER. - On handing over O.C.Coys will pay special attention to point out to their opposite numbers what work they have been doing re maintenance of trenches and all details about guards and sentries.

10. ACKNOWLEDGE.

                 signed   E.M.GREEFF.
                            Capt & Adjt.
                       2/24th Bn London Regt.

Order No 12   Appendix "2"

BATTALION ORDERS IN THE FIELD FOR TUESDAY 10/10/16.

by

Lieut. Colonel J.P.G.Crosbie, comdg
2/24th Battalion London Regiment.
The Queens.

---

1. **RELIEF.**   The Battalion will relieve the 2/22nd Battalion London Regiment in Right 11 on the 10th October 1916 as follows :-

   Signallers, Bombers, Lewis Gunners and Snipers will relieve in advance as detailed. Companies will commence relieving at 2.15 pm in the following order at the following times. Companies will move from ETRUN to ANZIN by platoons at 5 minutes interval - the leading platoon of "D" Coy. to reach ANZIN COMMUNICATION TRENCH by 3 pm.

   Companies will proceed to the trenches in the following order :-

           "D" Coy.
           "C" "
           "A" "
           "B" "

   DISPOSITIONS. - Dispositions will be as follows :-

       "D" Coy will relieve "C" Coy 2/22nd L.R. and will be on the right.

       "C" Coy will relieve "B" Coy 2/22nd L.R. and will be in the centre.

       "A" Coy will relieve "D" Coy 2/22nd L.R. and will be on the left.

       "B" Coy will relieve "A" Coy 2/22nd L.R. and will be in support.

   ROUTE.- Platoons must NOT halt in ANZIN. On no account will platoons or parties of platoons proceed across the open from ANZIN to MADAGASCAR. - The following route will be taken from ANZIN :-
   ANZIN AVENUE - the via ROCADE - HIGH STREET and LABYRINTHE.

2. **TRENCH STORES.** - O.C.Companies will detail 1 officer per company and their C.S.M. to proceed to the trenches during the morning and take over trench stores.

3. **REPORTS.** - On completion of relief O.C.Companies will report by wire in the following code -
   "APPLICATION RESUBMITTED TONIGHT"

4. **RUNNERS.** - NYNY Runners will be arranged by the Signalling Sergeant.

5. **CASUALTIES.** - Any casualties sustained during the relief will be reported in clear by runner to Battalion Headquarters.

6. **RATIONS.** - Times for sending Ration parties to the dumps will be notified later.

7. **ACKNOWLEDGE.**

                        E.M.GREEFF.
                        Capt & Adjutant,
                        2/24th Bn L.R.

Order No 13   15-10-16.

Battalion Orders
by
Lieut. Colonel J.P.C.Crosbie,
Cmmdg. 2/24th Battn. London Regiment,
The Queen's.

Appendix 3

---

1. **RELIEF.-** The Battalion will be relieved by the 2/22nd L.R. on 16-10-16 as follows, and will move into Brigade Reserve in "C" position. Relief will commence about 6.30 p.m.

2. Signallers, Bombers, Lewis Gunners, Snipers will be relieved in advance as detailed.

3. "A" Co. will be relieved by "D" Co. 2/22nd and move to ECURIE and relieve "B" Co. 2/21st.

   "B" Co. will be relieved by "C" Co. 2/22nd and will move to ABRI MOUTON and relieve "A" Co. 2/21st.

   "C" Co. will be relieved by "B" Co. 2/22nd and will move to SUNKEN ROAD and relieve "C" Co. 2/21st.

   "D" Co. will be relieved by "A" Co. 2/22nd and will move to ABRI CENTRALE and relieve "D" Co. 2/21st.

4. Coys. will move to their position by the usual communication trenches.

5. Coys. at SUNKEN ROAD - ABRI MOUTON will be under orders of O.C.Right II. Coy. at ABRI CENTRALE will be under order of O.C.Right I.

6. Maintenance of trenches. Before leaving Right II, O.C.Coys. will point out to their opposite numbers what work has been done and is being undertaken. On arrival in "C" position, O.C.Coys. will pay particular attention to take over all work concerning maintenance of communication trenches and will see that work is commenced the following day.

7. **TRENCHES STORES.-** Lists of stores duly signed by an Officer of the incoming and outgoing Coy. to be sent to Battn.H.Q. as soon as possible after handing over. Unsigned list of trench stores are to be sent to Battn.H.Q. as early as possible tomorrow morning.

8. **REPORTS.-** O.C.Coys. will report relief complete to Battn.H.Q. in the following code, by wire - "STATE TIME DUE".

9. **RUNNERS.-** Runners between Coy. and Battn.H.Q. in "C" position will be arranged by the Intercommunication Officer.

10. **REST.-** O.C.Coys. will make every endeavour to see that men obtain as much rest as possible.

11. **ACKNOWLEDGE.-**

(Sgd) E.M.GREEFF.
Captain & Adjutant,
2/24th Battalion London Regiment,
The Queen's.

15-10-16.

SECRET.   Copy No. 1
2/24th BATTALION LONDON REGIMENT.

Order No 14.   Appendix "4"

23/10/16. Ref Map LENS II Scale 1/100,000

1. **Relief.** - The Battalion will be relieved by the 4th Battalion Canadian Mounted Rifles on the 24th October 1916, as follows,- and will proceed to billets at MAROEUIL. A hot meal will be issued and there will be a short rest, after which the Battalion will march to IZEL LES HAMEAU. March orders will be issued separately. The Relief will commence at about 7.45 a.m.

2. Signallers and Lewis Gunners will be relieved in advance as detailed.

3. "A" Company will be relieved by "A" Company Canadian Mounted Rifles and will proceed to MAROEUIL via MADAGASCAR AVE, ANZIN AVE, and LOUEZ.

4. "B" Company will be relieved by "B" Company, Canadian Mounted Rifles, and will proceed to MAROEUIL via AVE MOUTON, GENIE AVE, ANZIN and LOUEZ.

5. "C" Company will be relieved by "C" Company, Canadian Mounted Rifles, and will proceed to MAROEUIL via ANNIVERSAIRE AVE, BETHUNE AVE, ANZIN, and LOUEZ.

6. "D" Company will be relieved by "D" Company, Canadian Mounted Rifles, and will proceed to MAROEUIL via BLANCHARD AVE, GENIE AVE, ANZIN, and LOUEZ.

7. Routes laid down to be strictly adhered to. No platoon is to leave its position in the line until properly relieved.

8. Guides to meet incoming platoons will be at ANZIN CHURCH at 6.45 a.m.. O/C. Companies will send one picked N.C.O. per platoon to act as guide. Lewis Gun Officer will send one guide per Lewis Gun team. Signalling Officer will send one guide for signallers and H.Q. details. Lieut. H.L.Rees will be in charge of all guides and will be held responsible that every N.C.O. and man detailed as a guide is fully aware of his duties. Guides will report to the Adjutant at 6.30 p.m. on 23/10/16 for further instructions.

9. Billeting Party of one N.C.O. per platoon and one N.C.O. for Headquarter Details will parade outside Bn. H.Q. TUNIS at 6.15 a.m. 24/10/16 under 2nd Lieut. H.L.Earle, who will proceed with party to MAROEUIL and report to Town Major's Office MAROEUIL at 8 a.m. Platoons will be met by N.C.O.s of billeting party on the MAROEUIL-LOUEZ Road and guided into billets. O.C.Companies will arrange direct with their C.Q.M.S.s for a hot meal to be served to the men directly they arrive in Billets.

10. O.C.Companies will establish an ALARM POST on arrival in Billets, the whereabouts to be notified to Battalion H.Q. A certificate stating that a hot meal has been issued will be sent to Bn. H.Q. One runner per Company will report to Bn. H.Q. by 9 a.m.

11. A list of Trench stores handed over - signed by the O.s C. of the incoming and outgoing Companies - will be handed in to Bn. H.Q. TUNIS.

12. O.C.Companies will select two picked N.C.O.s per Company, not below the rank of Corporal, to remain behind with the Company relieving them. The above personnel will report to the Staff Captain 8th Canadian Brigade, at Bde. H.Q. ETRUN at 10 a.m. 27/10/16, when they will proceed by lorry to rejoin their Unit. N.C.O.s selected to report to the Adjutant 6.30 p.m. 23/10/16.

P.T.O.

-2-

13. O.C.Companies will be careful to see that Dug-outs, Latrines, Refuse pits, etc., in their areas, are handed over in a clean condition.

14. Completion of relief will be reported to Bn. H.Q. in the following code.-

"FOR FURTHER PARTICULARS SEE SMALL HAND BILLS"

15. Acknowledge.

E. M. Eee B.
Capt. and Adjt.,
2/24th Batt. London Regt.,

Copies issued.-

1. War Diary.
2. O.C. 4th Canadian Mtd. Rifles.
3. 181st Inf. Bde.
4. O.C. "A" Coy.
5. "   "B" "
6. "   "C" "
7. "   "D" "
8. Quartermaster.
9. Transport Officer.
10. Lewis Gun Officer.
11. Signalling Officer.

SECRET.   Copy No. 2......

                                                       Appendix 5

                    2/24th Battn London Regiment.

                         March Order No 15.

23rd October 1916.   Ref Map. LENS 11 1/100,000.
                                                 FRANCE 51c 1/40,000.

_____

1. The Battalion including Transport (Echelon A & B) will march from
   MAROEUIL to IZEL LES HAMEAU on the 24th October 1916. Route via
   HABARCQ.

2. Coys will proceed by platoons 100 yards interval between each platoon
   to the fork Road above the E in LARESSET on the ETRUN - HERMAVILLE
   Road. Coys will leave MAROEUIL in the following order, A. B. C. D.
   time of starting to be notified later. On arrival at the above point
   platoons will halt and the Battn will be formed up into column of route

3. Transport will proceed in rear of Coys 200 yards between vehicles to the
   point mentioned in para 2 and form up in column of route in rear of
   the Battn. Time of starting to be notified later.

4. Billeting party will leave in advance. Officer i/c to meet Battn on
   arrival in billets. Guides for Coys to be detailed in readiness to
   conduct the Coys to billets.

5. On arrival in billets O.C.Coys will render certificates and returns
   to Battn H.Q. without delay as laid down in Battn Standing Orders for
   billets para 11.

6. A Coy will detail 1 platoon as inlying picquet.

7. O.C.Coys will see that all points laid down in "Memorandum on the
   subject of march discipline" issued by 181st Inf Bde receives special
   attention.

8. General Routine Order that all ranks are to wear the Steel Helmets on
   the line of march and that it is not permitted to carry the helmet on
   the pack is to be strictly enforced.

9. ACKNOWLEDGE.

                                            Capt & Adjt.
                                       2/24th Battn London Regiment.

Copies issued to
 No 1. 181st Inf Bde.
    2 War Diary.
    3. O.C. "A" Coy.
    4. O.C. "B" Coy.
    5. O.C. "C" Coy.
    6. O.C. "D" Coy.
    7. Quartermaster.
    8. Transport Officer.

SECRET   COPY NO.

           2/24th Battalion London Regiment,   Appendix "5"
                 The Queen's.

           AFTER ORDER TO MARCH ORDER No.15.

24th October 1916.
     Ref.Map. LENS II. 1/100,000   France 51 c.
                                              1/40,500.

---

1. Reference Para 2 of March Order No.15, copy No.   issued to you.
   time of starting and order of starting as follows.-

      No.1 Platoon of "A" Co. will leave billets at 2.30 p.m.
      No.5 Platoon of "B" Co. will leave billets at 2.35 p.m.
      No.9 Platoon of "C" Co. will leave billets at 2.40 p.m.
      No.13 Platoon of "D" Co. will leave billets at 2.45 p.m.

2. The following order is to be communicated to all ranks before
   starting. Chin Straps will be worn round the back of the head
   and as far as possible must be made to fit properly. The order
   that all ranks are to wear Chin Straps under the chin is hereby
   cancelled, and the above substituted.

3. On arrival at starting point O.C. "D" Co. will detail one platoon, under
   an Officer, to march in rear of the Battn, keeping at a distance
   of 200 yards. The duties of this platoon will be.-

      (a) Pick up all stragglers and make them march as a body with
          this Platoon.
      (b) The Officer i/c will stop all men falling out and if they
          are not in possession of a chit from the M.O. granting
          them permission to ride on the Ambulance, will order them
          to fall in with this platoon as directed above.

                                        (Sgd) E.N.GREEFF.
                                        2/24th Battn. London Regt.,
                                             The Queen's.

Copies issued to.

O.C. "A" Co.
     "B" Co.
     "C" Co.
     "D" Co.

Appendix 6

SECRET.   Copy..........

2/24th Battn London Regiment.

March Order No 16.

24th October 1916.   Ref Map. LENS 11 1/100,000.
                                               FRANCE 51c 1/40,000.

---

1. The Battalion including Transport (Echelon A & B) will march from IZEL LES HAMEAU to MAIZERES on 25th October 1916. Route via PENIN.

2. Starting Point, time and place of parade to be notified later.

3. Billeting party will leave in advance. Officer i/c to meet Battn on arrival in billets. Guides for Coys to be detailed in readiness to conduct Coys to billets.

4. On arrival in billets O.C.Coys will render certificates and returns to Battn H.Q. without delay as laid down in Battalion Standing Orders for billets para 11.

5. B Coy will detail one platoon for inlying picquet.

6. O.C.Coys will see that all points laid down in "Memorandum on the subject of March Discipline" issued by 181st Inf Bde receive special attention.

7. General Routine Order that all ranks are to wear the Steel Helmet on the line of march, and that it is not permitted to carry the Helmet on the pack, is to be strictly enforced.

8. ACKNOWLEDGE.

                                        Capt & Adjt.
                                        2/24th Battn London Regiment.

Copies issued to
No 1 181st Inf Bde.
   2 War Diary.
   3 O.C. "A" Coy.
   4 O.C. "B" Coy.
   5 O.C. "C" Coy.
   6 O.C. "D" Coy.
   7 Quartermaster.
   8 Transport Officer.

Appendix 6.

SECRET.   Copy No 2.

2/24th Battalion London Regiment.

After Order to March Order No 16.

24th October 1916.
   Ref Map Lens 11. 1/100,000.   France 51c.
                                  1/40,000.

1. Para 1 amend as follows:-
   Delete "MAIZIERES" and substitute
   "BEAUDRICOURT".
   Delete "PENIN" and substitute "via MANIN –
   LIENCOURT - ETREE-WAMIN".

2. Para 3 add the following :-
   Billeting party will meet the Assistant
   Staff Captain at MAIRIE, BEAUDRICOURT at
   11 am.

                    signed   E.M.GREEFF.
                             Capt & Adjt.
                             2/24th Battn London Regt.

Copies issued to
   No 1. 181st Inf Bde.
      2. War Diary.   7. Quartermaster.
      3. O.C. "A" Coy.   8. Transport Officer.
      4. O.C. "B" Coy.
      5. O.C. "C" Coy.
      6. O.C. "C" Coy.

Copy No 2.

2/24th Battalion London Regiment.

After Order to March Order No 16.

Ref Map, Lens 11 1/100,000. France 51c
1/40,000.

The Battalion including Transport Echelons "A" & "B" will parade in column of Route in the following order -

      H.Q.Signals.
      C. Company.
      D. do
      A. do
      B. do

on the IZEL LES HAMEAU - MANIN ROAD at 10 am. Head of the column to be at a point on this road 200 yards below the "U" in IZEL LES HAMEAU.

          signed E.M.GREEFF.
          Capt & Adjt.
Copies to   2/24th Bn. London Regt.
No 1. 181st Inf Bde.
   2 War Diary.
   3 O.C. "A" Coy.   7. Quartermaster.
   4 O.C. "B" Coy.   8. Transport Officer.
   5 O.C. "C" Coy.
   7 O.C. "D" Coy.

Appendix "Y"

SECRET.   Copy No. *Adjt.*

2/24th Battalion London Regiment,
The Queen's.

27-10-16.   March Order No. 17.

_____

1. The Battalion, including Transport (Echelon "A" & "B"), will march from BEAUDRICOURT to BARLY on 28th October 1916.
Route.- BEAUDRICOURT, LE SOUICH - BOUQUEMAISON - NEUVILLETTE - BARLY.

2. The Battalion will be formed up in column of route on the BEAUDRICOURT - IVERGNY ROAD by 9 a.m. in the following order.-

   H.Q.Signallers, "D" Co. "A" Co. "B" Co. "C" Co. Lewis Gun Handcarts and Transport. Head of the column to be at the Brewery. O.C."C" Co. will detail 1 platoon to march in rear of the column.

3. BAGGAGE.- Blankets, rolled in bundles of 10, will be taken round to the Quartermaster Stores and stacked by 6.30 a.m.
   Officers valises will be at Quartermaster stores ready for loading by 6.45 a.m.

4. BILLETING PARTY.- Billeting Party as detailed will leave in advance and will report to Monsieur Odrent at 9 a.m. at the Mairie, BARLY. O.C.N.COs. mounted on bicycles, will report to 2nd.Lieut. F.P.Wright, at Battalion H.Q. at 6.45 a.m.

5. On arrival in Billets, O.C.Coys. will render certificates and returns to Battn.H.Q. without delay as laid down in Battalion Standing Orders for Billets. 1 Runner per Coy. must be sent to Battn.H.Q. immediately on arrival.

6. MARCH DISCIPLINE.- The following orders must be strictly adhered to.-
   At the regulation halts, N.C.O's. and men must remove their packs.
   On the march the top button of the tunic will be kept undone.
   No smoking at all on the march, except at halts.
   All points laid down in Memorandum on March Discipline issued by 181st Inf. Bde. must receive special attention.

7. ACKNOWLEDGE.

                                        [signature]
                                        Captain & Adjutant,
                                        2/24th Battalion London Regiment,
                                        The Queen's.
Battn.H.Q.
27th October 1916.

Copies Issued to

No.1 181st Inf.Bde.
   2 War Diary.
   3 O.C. "A" Co.
   4 O.C. "B" Co.
   5 O.C. "C" Co.
   6 O.C. "D" Co.
   7 Signalling Officer.
   8 Transport Officer.
   9 Quartermaster.

SECRET   Copy No.

2/24th Battalion London Regiment, *Appendix 8.*
The Queen's.

28-10-16.   March Order No.18.   Ref.Map. LENS 11.
                                                                          1/100,000.

---

1. The Battalion including Transport (echelon "A" & "B") will march from BARLY to FIENVILLERS on the 29th October 1916. Route – OUTREBOIS – LE QUESNEL FARM – BOIS BERGUES.

2. The Battalion will be formed up in column of route on the BARLY – OUTREBOIS ROAD, head of column opposite Battn.H.Q. The Mairie, by 7.45 a.m. in the following order.-
Hdqrts.Sigs. "A", "B", "C", "D", Stretcher Bearers, Lewis Gun Handcarts and Transport. O.C. "D" Co. will detail 1 Platoon to march in rear of the column.

3. BAGGAGE. Blankets rolled in bundles of 10 will be taken round to the Q.M.Stores by 6 a.m. Officers Valises will be at the Q.M.Stores ready for loading by 6.30 a.m. The Orderly Officer will supervise the loading of baggage at the Q.M.Stores at 6 a.m. O.C. "C" Co. will detail 1 Cpl. and 4 men to report to the Q.M.Stores at 6.45 a.m. to proceed with a lorry in advance.

4. All stretchers bearers will march in rear of the Battalion behind the Lewis Gunners and will be under direct command of the Medical Officer. Stretchers will be carried in the Maltese Cart, which will be in rear of the stretcher bearers squad.

5. DRESS.   Mess tins must be carried in the pack and not slung outside. Iron Rations must be carried in the haversack and not tied on the equipment.

6. BILLETING PARTY. Billeting Party, as detailed, will report to the Billeting Officer at the Q.M.Stores at 6.45 a.m. and report to the Town Major's Office, CANDAS, to get all necessary information re billets in FIENVILLERS.

7. On arrival in billets, O.C.Coys. will render the usual certificates to Battn.H.Q. 1 runner per Coy. must be sent to Battn.H.Q. immediately on arrival.

8. *Acknowledge.*

                                                                 [signature]
                                                             Captain & Adjutant,
                                                      2/24th Battalion London Regiment,
                                                                  The Queen's.

Battn.H.Q.
28th October 1916.

Copies issued to.

No. 1.   181st Inf.Bde.
    2.   War Diary.
    3.   O.C. "A" Co.
    4.   O.C. "B" Co.
    5.   O.C. "C" Co.
    6.   O.C. "D" Co.
    7.   Signalling Officer.
    8.   Transport Officer.
    9.   Quartermaster.
  10.   Medical Officer.

181st Brigade.
60th Division.

> Preparing for move to SALONIKA

2/24th BATTALION

LONDON REGIMENT

NOVEMBER 1916.

2/24th London Regiment

The Queen's.

War Diary   Volume No I

Copy No 6.

November 1916

WAR DIARY
2/24th London Regt or 1st Queens
INTELLIGENCE SUMMARY
(Erase heading not required.)

Army Form C. 2118

Instructions regarding War Diaries and Intelligence Summaries are contained in F.S. Regs., Part II. and the Staff Manual respectively. Title Pages will be prepared in manuscript.

Place	Date	Hour	Summary of Events and Information	Remarks and references to Appendices
PIENVILLERS	1/11/16		The Battalion carried out General training including Physical Drill, Plan & Gun Drill, Arms Practice and Entrenching Digging also Bayonet fighting.	Ap.
do.	2/11/16		ditto	Ap.
do.	3/11/16		ditto	Ap.
do.	4/11/16	8.35 A.M.	The Battalion commenced entraining transport to MOUFLERS and VAUCHELLES-LES-DOMART. H.Q. Transport, "A" & "B" Companies billeting at MOUFLERS. "C" & "D" Companies at VAUCHELLES-LES-DOMART.	See Appendix Ap. 1.
MOUFLERS. VAUCHELLES.	5/11/16	6.30 A.M.	Companies carried out drill. The Battalion attended Divine Service. Services being partly spoiled during the afternoon.	Ap.
do.	6/11/16		The Battalion went out on several training exercises. Bayonet fighting, Rapid loading etc.	Ap.
do.	7/11/16		Physical exercises in morning followed by company drill in the afternoon until tea time.	Ap.
do.	8/11/16		Battalion went out on a General training. Sent out party to work on ranges. Bayonet fighting, Lewis Gun Instruction, Signalling etc.	Ap.

Army Form C. 2118

WAR DIARY
2/24th London Regt or The Queens
INTELLIGENCE SUMMARY
(Erase heading not required.)

Instructions regarding War Diaries and Intelligence Summaries are contained in F. S. Regs., Part II. and the Staff Manual respectively. Title Pages will be prepared in manuscript.

Place	Date	Hour	Summary of Events and Information	Remarks and references to Appendices
MOULLERS. VAUCHELLES.	9/1/16	9.30 a.m.	Reorganisation parade for Revd. Blenerd. Kerring Chief Genoa. Lt-Col. Flatten & Officers. Service, improving lights & Latrines digging continued.	
"	10/1/16		General training.	
"	11/1/16		General training.	
"	12/1/16	10.30 a.m.	Reorganisation at Divine Service.	
"				
"	13/1/16		General Training.	
"	14/1/16		General training. Platoon practice attack during the afternoon.	
"	15/1/16		Received training. Using Lys Cylinders.	
"	16/1/16		General training, interior economy. Absorbing (Trench fighting, instruction with live bombs, new phones issued 2.30 p.m.)	

1875 W.L. W593/526 1,000,000 4/15 J.B.C. & A. A.D.S.S./Forms/C. 2118.

… **WAR DIARY**
1/2th London Regt. 2nd Lieut.
INTELLIGENCE SUMMARY
(Erase heading not required.)

Army Form C. 2118

Place	Date	Hour	Summary of Events and Information	Remarks and references to Appendices
MOUFLERS	17/11/16		Battalion carried out General training including extended order drill. Divisional heavies. Co-operation drivers outing afternoon	[sig]
VAUCHELLES	18/11/16		ditto. A Medley Race took place at 10.30 am	[sig]
"	19/11/16		Service held at 7.30, 11.30 am at VAUCHELLES + 10.30 am at MOUFLERS	[sig]
"	20/11/16		Companies carried out route march morning. Support drill reviewed Bn. drill evening afternoon	[sig]
"	21/11/16		General training including attacking formations Lewis gun topics etc	[sig]
"	22/11/16		ditto	[sig]
"	23/11/16		General training including route march during morning	[sig]
"	24/11/16		General training	[sig]

WAR DIARY
2/4th London Regt / Lt Dunn
INTELLIGENCE SUMMARY

Army Form C. 2118

(Erase heading not required.)

Instructions regarding War Diaries and Intelligence Summaries are contained in F.S. Regs., Part II. and the Staff Manual respectively. Title Pages will be prepared in manuscript.

Place	Date	Hour	Summary of Events and Information	Remarks and references to Appendices
MOUFLERS	24/6/16		"A" & "B" Companies paraded at 8 am and marched to LONGPRÉ where they entrained at 10 am and left at 1.15 pm en route for MARSEILLES	See Appendix 1, 2
VAUCHELLES	25/6/16		"C" & "D" Companies. H.Qrs. Transport paraded at 11.45 am and marched to LONGPRÉ where they entrained at and left at for MARSEILLES	
	26/6/16		In route for MARSEILLES	
	27/6/16		"A" & "B" Companies arrived at MARSEILLES and marched to MUSSO CAMP arriving at 6 pm	
	28/6/16		"C" & "D" Companies. H.Qrs. Transport arrived at MARSEILLES and disembarked at "THE BRAJEURIE" at 8 pm. "A" & "B" Companies carried on General Training in Camp	
MARSEILLES	29/6/16		The Battalion marched out General Training in Camp	
	30/6/16		"A" "B" "C" & "D" Companies carried on General Training in Camp. "C" & "D" Companies joined "A" & "B" Companies in MUSSO CAMP at 10.30 am	

for Lieut Colonel Commdg
2/4th London Regt

SECRET.   COPY No. 1

2/24th Batt. London Regiment The Queen's.   *Appendix 1.*

MARCH ORDER NO. 19.

3/11/16.   Ref. Maps. LENS 11,
                                                                                 ABBEVILLE 14,
                                                                                    1/100,000.

---

1. The Battalion including Transport (Echelon "A" & "B") will march from FIENVILLERS to MOUFLERS and VAUCHELLES - LES - DOMART, on the 4th November 1916. Headquarters, Transport, "A" and "B" Companies to MOUFLERS, "C" and "D" Companies to VAUCHELLES-Les-DOMART. Route.- BERNEUIL and DOMART- EN- PONTHIEU.

2. The Battalion will be formed up in Column of Route in the following order.- H.Q.Sigs., "B", "A", "D", and "C" Companies, Stretcher Bearers, Lewis Gun Handcarts, and Transport, on the FIENVILLERS-BERNEUIL Road by 8.25 a.m. Head of Column to be at Road Junction W. end of FIENVILLERS.

3. Baggage,- Blankets rolled in bundles of 10 will be taken round to the Q.M.Stores at 6.30 a.m. sharp. The Battalion Orderly Officer will supervise the loading of blanket wagon and other baggage wagons at the Q.M.Stores at 6.30 a.m. Officers' valises and Company Stationery boxes must be at the Q.M.Stores ready for loading by 6.30 a.m.

4. Billeting Party.- Billeting Party as detailed will proceed in advance by lorry and will report to the Q.M.Stores at 7.a.m. proceed to MOUFLERS, and report to the Billeting Officer at the Church.

5. Before leaving Billets, O.C.Companies will send certificates to the Adjutant certifiying that billets have been left clean.

6. On arrival in billets, O.C.Companies will render the usual returns and certificates to the Adjutant.
O.C.Companies will detail one runner per Company to report to Battalion H.Q. on arrival in billets, who has previously without fail ascertained the whereabouts of Company H.Q. "C" and "D" Company runners will be provided with bicycles.

7. ACKNOWLEDGE.

                                                     Capt. and Adjt.,
                                             2/24th Battalion London Regt.,

Copies to.-

1. File.
2. 181st Bde.
3. War Diary.
4. O.C."A" Coy.
5. " "B" "
6. " "C" "
7. " "D" "
8. Signalling Officer.
9. Billeting Officer.
10. Transport Officer.
11. Quartermaster.
12. Medical Officer.

Appendix 2

2/24th Battalion London Regiment, The Queen's.

MOVE ORDER NO. 20

The Battalion will entrain at LONGPRE on 25th November 1916.

"A" & "B" Coys. H Q Signallers, H Q Bombers and personel of Transport as detailed by Transport Officer will parade under Major J A McAnally at LA Folie at 8 a m. This party will travel by train due to start at 10 27 a m. Lewis Gun & Sniping Officers will be at disposal of O C "B" Coy. for duty during the journey.

H Q Signallers and H Q Bombers will be under orders of Bombing Officer.

"C" & "D" Coys, remainder of Transport Section, Quarter guard and prisoners will parade at junction of MOUFLERS - FLIXECOURT, and MOUFLERS - BOUCHON ROADS at 11 45 a m. This party will be under Command of the Commanding Officer and will catch the train due to leave LONGPRE at 2 17 p m.

O C "A" & "D" Coys. will each detail 1 Officer and 2 N C O's. as advance parties. These must each report to R T O. at LONGPRE 3 hours before their respective trains are due to start. Loading parties will be found from staff of Quartermaster.

Baggage which has not been deposited at Q M Stores by 4 a m. will have to be carried.

Each man will carry his own blanket rolled bandolier fashion.

Horses will travel under arrangements made by Transport Officer. Not more than 10 being in first train and not more than 14 in second. Those to travel in first train must be at the station by 7 30 a m. and those to travel in second by 11 15 a m.

2nd Lieut & Acting Adjutant,
2/24th Battalion London Regiment,
The Queen's.

Copies issued to.

No		
1	File.	
2	H Q 181st Inf Bde.	
3	War Diary.	
4	O C "A" Coy.	
5	" "B" Coy.	
6	" "C" Coy.	
7	" "D" Coy.	
8	Quartermaster.	
9	O C Transport.	
10	Lewis Gun Officer.	
11	Signalling Officer.	
12	Bombing Officer.	

www.ingramcontent.com/pod-product-compliance
Lightning Source LLC
Chambersburg PA
CBHW081442160426
43193CB00013B/2362